The READY RESOURCE *for* RELIEF SOCIETY

The READY RESOURCE *for* RELIEF SOCIETY

THE TEACHINGS OF

GEORGE ALBERT SMITH

compiled by

TRINA BOICE

CFI

An Imprint of Cedar Fort, Inc.

Springville, Utah

ISBN 13: 978-1-59955-930-8

Published by CFI, an imprint of Cedar Fort, Inc., 2373 W. 700 S., Springville, UT, 84663
Distributed by Cedar Fort, Inc., www.cedarfort.com

Cover and book design by Danie Romrell
Cover design © 2011 by Lyle Mortimer
Edited by Kelley Konzak

Printed in the United States of America

10 9 8 7 6 5 4 3 2

Printed on acid-free paper

CONTENTS

ACKNOWLEDGMENTS

Thank you to Cedar Fort for inviting me to share this book adventure with them! A big thank you to my wonderfully supportive family for taking care of everything around me while I was busy pounding away at my keyboard writing this book!

Thank you to all the faithful members of the Church who valiantly magnify their callings and give of their time and talents to bless those around them. Not only should we read the scriptures and have a meaningful gospel study plan, but we're also commanded to feast on the scriptures! It is my hope that this book serves as helpful utensils to enjoy your meal!

INTRODUCTION

The Ready Resource for Relief Society for 2012 is designed to be a helpful, inspiring resource to make lesson preparation easier and more exciting. Each chapter includes hymns appropriate for the lesson, quick summaries of the lesson material, quotes to supplement your class discussions, suggested artwork to display during your presentation, video suggestions, and object lessons to add pizzazz to your student participation. In addition, each chapter contains a space to take personal notes as you prepare your thoughts and a handout to share with your class. Each handout equals the same size as half a sheet of paper, so copying is quick and easy. The most important tool is the Holy Ghost, which will help you to tailor each lesson to meet the needs of your sisters!

Integrating various learning styles into your lessons improves retention and attention, assists in lesson planning, and inspires participants. Everyone learns differently, so be sure to include lots of variety in your teaching techniques. Try using some of the following ideas during your lessons:

STUDENT CENTERED

- Assignments
- Brainstorming
- Case Study
- Crafts
- Discussion (general, panel, small groups)
- Instructional Games
- Memorizing
- Note Taking
- Oral Reading
- Role-Playing
- Singing
- Testimonies
- Worksheets

MATERIALS CENTERED
Bulletin Board
Chalkboard
Charts and Maps
Displays
Dramatization
Flip Chart
Flash Cards
Flannel Board
DVD
Overhead Transparency
Pictures
Posters
Puppet Show
Tape Recording

TEACHER CENTERED
Guest Speaker
Jokes and Puns
Lecture
Oral Reading
Storytelling
Summarizing
Testimony

ARTWORK: Beautiful artwork can teach in a way that words alone cannot. The Church's new Gospel Art Book is wonderful and can be purchased through Church distribution inexpensively. It makes a terrific addition to your family home evening lessons too! The book includes 137 pictures that depict scripture or Church history events and illustrate gospel principles in action. They're organized into the following categories:

1. Old Testament
2. New Testament
3. Book of Mormon
4. Church History
5. Gospel in Action
6. Latter-day Prophets

You can view and download the images at www.gospelart.lds.org or watch the Church's promotional video at LDSMediaTalk. Other terrific Church resources that provide excellent artwork on gospel themes can be found at:

www.images.lds.org — LDS images

www.lds.org/hf/art/0,16812,4218-1,00.html — Gospel Art Kit
http://lib.byu.edu/digital/relarchive/ — BYU religious education image archive
josephsmith.net — Joseph Smith Resource Center (maps, artwork, photos, documents, and more!)
scriptures.lds.org/en/biblephotos/contents — Photographs of scriptural sites
scriptures.lds.org/en/chphotos/contents — Photographs of Church History sites

MUSIC: Music can effectively teach and invite the Spirit almost better than any other teaching technique. Included with each lesson are suggestions for songs the class could sing or simply learn from by reading the lyrics. Inviting others in your ward to provide special musical numbers during your lessons binds hearts together and uplifts everyone. You can find the LDS hymnbook online at http://www.lds.org/churchmusic.

Download songs, listen to them online, and do searches by topics, titles, and even scriptures! You can also use songs from seminary, Young Women, and Primary, and music that has been published in Church magazines. Also on the Church's website are learning materials, such as how to conduct music, how to understand symbols and terms, and where to find great ideas to add variety to singing.

QUOTES: Quotes from Church authorities can inspire the mind and heart. It's nice to have some quotes written on the board at the front of the room for students to read before class starts. They can set the tone and get the students thinking about the topic. Some of the suggested handouts in this book use such quotes, but you can also design your own, using your favorite quotes. More can be found online at:

www.quotegarden.com
www.thinkexist.com
www.inspirational-quotes.info
www.brainyquote.com

ENSIGN ARTICLES: What a blessing to read from Church leaders each month in the various Church magazines. Teach your class how to find material they can share during family home evening lessons or sacrament talks. Each lesson in this book includes only a few suggested *Ensign* articles, but there are many more! In preparing for your lessons, you will be blessed if you spend time researching specific gospel topics. You will learn so much more than you'll ever have time to share with your students in class on Sunday! Teaching Relief Society is a wonderful excuse to truly immerse yourself in gospel study. Enjoy it!

OBJECT LESSONS: Object lessons capture students' interest and increase understanding by teaching the concept in a unique way. The Savior often used physical objects that were familiar to His listeners to illustrate simple principles. Each lesson offers ideas for object lessons that could be an effective introduction to the topic or a fun way to keep the class engaged.

VIDEOS: The Church has some excellent videos that have been made for seminary and family home evening. They also have many inspirational clips called "Mormon Messages" on YouTube. Be sure to visit the Church's website section that is dedicated to Relief Society resources at www.lds.org. Click on "Serving in the Church" and then "Relief Society." The section entitled "Sunday Relief Society Meetings" has been created just for you and this sacred calling! The steps suggested for how to prepare a lesson include:

Use approved lesson materials.
Seek the guidance of the Spirit.
Study your lesson in advance.
Consider the needs of your sisters.
Organize the lesson.
Seek the gift of teaching.

Jesus was the Master teacher. He still is! He cared deeply about each person He taught. He used variety, honesty, symbolism, and storytelling.

He challenged listeners to make specific changes in their lives. The more you study and teach the gospel, the greater will be your own understanding.

Use the scriptures each time you teach, and encourage your class to sup from their pages. As you come to love the scriptures, your class will feel that passion and be inspired to feast upon them as well. Your task as a teacher is to invite your sisters to "come unto Christ." In order to do that effectively, you must create an atmosphere where the Holy Ghost is welcome and can testify to the hearts of your students. You give voice to the gospel principles taught each week, but the Holy Ghost will touch hearts and transform lives through testifying. May you feel the Savior's love as you feed His sheep!

LESSON ONE
LIVING WHAT WE BELIEVE

Hymns

"Father in Heaven, We Do Believe" — Hymns #180
"I Believe in Being Honest" — Children's Songbook #149
"I Believe in Christ" — Hymns #134
"Nephi's Courage" — Children's Songbook #120
"Sweet Is the Peace the Gospel Brings" — Hymns #14

SUMMARY:

Religion isn't just something we believe; it is truly the blueprint for how we live our daily lives. President George Albert Smith wrote down his personal creed for living: eleven rules based on gospel principles that guided his behavior until the day he died. The gospel of Jesus Christ isn't about learning interesting scriptural facts or debating doctrine; rather, it is about applying those principles to our behavior and becoming Christlike in all that we say and do. Heavenly Father cares more about who we are than what we know.

Integrity is doing what you know to be true. Hypocrisy is when we go to church one day and act like nonbelievers the other six days of the week. We can't live worldly lives and then expect heavenly rewards. As members of the Church, we are expected to learn the gospel, live it, and share it. It should be our goal to progress from knowing to doing to becoming.

QUOTES:

- "As disciples of the Savior, we are not merely striving to know more; rather, we need to consistently do more of what we know is right and become better. We should remember that bearing a heartfelt testimony is only a beginning. We need to bear testimony, we need to mean it, and most importantly we need consistently to live it. We need to both declare and live our testimonies" (David A. Bednar, "More Diligent and Concerned at Home," *Ensign*, Nov. 2009, 17).
- "True doctrine, understood, changes attitudes and behavior. The study of the doctrines of the gospel will improve behavior quicker than a study of behavior will improve behavior" (Boyd K. Packer, "Little Children," *Ensign*, Nov. 1986).
- "If a person understands the teachings of Jesus, he or she cannot reasonably conclude that our loving Heavenly Father or His divine Son believes that Their love supersedes Their commandments. . . . The effect of God's commandments and laws is not changed to accommodate popular behavior or desires" (Dallin H. Oaks, "Love and Law," *Ensign*, Nov. 2009, 28).

GOSPEL ART:

Sermon on the Mount – 212
The Anti-Nephi-Lehies Burying Their Swords – 311
Family Prayer – 606
Serving One Another – 615
Search the Scriptures – 617
The Articles of Faith – 618

VIDEOS:

- "We Believe: Theme Song," http://lds.org/media-library/video/strength-of-youth-media?lang=eng
- "You're Not Alone," http://www.youtube.com/watch?v=LjHZxjfxUmU&feature=youtube_gdata
- Check out all the wonderful video testimonies at www.mormon.org/people.

OBJECT LESSONS:

- Use a magician's repeat change bag (a change bag with three compartments). Make three signs that say "LOVE" on strips of thin fabric, putting one in each compartment.

  Tell the class that God loves all of us but that we have to receive His love. Ask a volunteer to reach into the bag. She'll pull out the first "LOVE" sign and show it to the class. Then explain that some people think that God couldn't possibly love them because they've done such terrible things. Show the empty bag compartment. Tell the class that God never runs out of love, and while He doesn't love our sins, He will always love us. While talking, secretly switch compartments and invite another sister to reach into the bag, pulling out the second "LOVE" sign and showing it to the class.

  Next show the empty compartment and mention that sometimes we get angry with God or push Him away because of our trials. Switch compartments again and talk about how we often begin with a testimony but then treat the gospel casually and wonder why we don't feel God's presence anymore. Invite another sister to reach into the bag, pulling out the third "LOVE" sign. God's love is always there!

❧ If:

A B C D E F G H I J K L M N O P Q R S T U V W X Y Z

is represented as:

1 2 3 4 5 6 7 8 9 10 11 12 13 14 15 16 17 18 19 20 21 22 23 24 25 26

Then:

H-A-R-D-W-O-R-K

8+1+18+4+23+15+18+11 = 98%

And:

K-N-O-W-L-E-D-G-E

11+14+15+23+12+5+4+7+5 = 96%

But:

A-T-T-I-T-U-D-E

1+20+20+9+20+21+4+5 = 100%

Look how far the love of God will take you:

L-O-V-E-O-F-G-O-D

12+15+22+5+15+6+7+15+4 = 101%

Therefore, one can conclude with mathematical certainty that: While hard work and knowledge will get you close, and attitude will get you there, it's the love of God that will put you over the top! We do our part, and the Lord will add His part!

ENSIGN ARTICLES:

John W. Welch and David J. Whittaker, "'We Believe. . . .': Development of the Articles of Faith," Sept. 1979

Henry B. Eyring, "A Living Testimony," May 2011

Howard W. Hunter, "Am I a Living Member?" May 1987

NOTES:

As disciples of the Savior, we are not merely striving to know more; *rather,* we need to consistently do more of what we know is right and become better.

David A. Bednar

As disciples of the Savior, we are not merely striving to know more; *rather,* we need to consistently do more of what we know is right and become better.

David A. Bednar

LESSON TWO

"LOVE THY NEIGHBOUR AS THYSELF"

Hymns

"Because I Have Been Given Much" — Hymns #219
"Love One Another" — Hymns #308
"'Tis Sweet to Sing the Matchless Love" — Hymns #177
"We Have Partaken of Thy Love" — Hymns #155

SUMMARY:

How can you tell a true disciple of Jesus Christ? By the way she treats other people! One way we show the Lord how much we love Him is by serving His children, our brothers and sisters. When we feel God's love deep inside our souls, we feel a desire to reach outside ourselves and bless others. A true understanding of the gospel of Jesus Christ compels us to love and serve.

If we want to be like Christ, we need to do as Christ did: serve. The Savior ministered daily to the needs of those around Him. When we open our spiritual eyes, we will see many opportunities around us for Christlike service and love. Loving and serving our neighbor isn't always easy, but that great feeling you get afterward is evidence that you're doing exactly what the Savior would do!

QUOTES:

- “We ought to be full of charity, of brotherly kindness and affection and love one towards another and love towards all men. We ought to feel as our Heavenly Father does” (John Taylor, *Teachings of the Presidents of the Church: John Taylor*).

- “Love is what inspired our Heavenly Father to create our spirits; it is what led our Savior to the Garden of Gethsemane to make Himself a ransom for our sins. Love is the grand motive of the plan of salvation; it is the source of happiness, the ever-renewing spring of healing, the precious fountain of hope.

  “As we extend our hands and hearts toward others in Christlike love, something wonderful happens to us. Our own spirits become healed, more refined, and stronger. We become happier, more peaceful, and more receptive to the whisperings of the Holy Spirit” (Dieter F. Uchtdorf, “‘You Are My Hands,’” *Ensign*, May 2010, 70, 75).

- “The more we serve our fellowmen in appropriate ways, the more substance there is to our souls” (Spencer W. Kimball, “President Kimball Speaks Out on Service to Others,” *New Era*, Mar. 1981, 47–49).

GOSPEL ART:

Christ Healing a Blind Man – 213
Christ and the Children – 216
The Good Samaritan – 218
Jesus Washing the Apostles’ Feet – 226
King Benjamin Addresses His People – 307
Alma Baptizes in the Waters of Mormon – 309
The Prophet Joseph Loved Children – 420
Serving One Another – 615

VIDEOS:

- "Choose This Day," www.lds.org/ldsorg/v/index.jsp?vgnextoid=bd163ca6e9aa3210VgnVCM1000003a94610aRCRD&locale=0
- "Love Thy Neighbor," http://www.youtube.com/watch?v=lq5IzDW4ufA
- "Flecks of Gold," http://ldsvideoblog.com/lds-movie/beliefs
- "Charity: An Example of the Believers," http://www.youtube.com/watch?v=A-ih_ZkaKC0&feature=youtube_gdata
- "For Madison," http://www.youtube.com/watch?v=kpe-n5LdTks&feature=youtube_gdata
- "We Believe in Doing Good to All Men: Service," http://www.youtube.com/watch?v=VXdTNEri1GE&feature=youtube_gdata

OBJECT LESSONS:

- Get eight cups that fit into each other. Read 2 Peter 2:5 and label each of your cup layers according to the things Paul talks about, starting with faith and ending with charity at the top. Then read 1 Corinthians 13:4 and label sixteen Popsicle sticks with each one of the descriptions of charity. Glue a little flower to the top of each Popsicle stick, and you now have a cute flower arrangement that shows how we go from faith to charity!
- While teaching your lesson, remove your jacket, belt, shoes and unbutton some buttons on your sleeves, without explaining why. At the end say "You probably won't remember a word I said by the time you get home, but you will never forget what I did. Actions speak louder than words."

- Teach the sisters how to knit or crochet so that during your lesson they can begin making leper bandages to send to LDS Charities. Go to the Church's Humanitarian Services website for specific instructions, as well as for more great service ideas: http://lds.org/service/humanitarian

- Pass around a mirror and ask the sisters to look in it. Ask them if when they focused on their own image they were able to see anyone else. (No.) By serving others, we focus less on our own problems and challenges and gain improved perspective.

ENSIGN ARTICLES:

Robert J. Matthews, "What 'Loving Your Neighbor' Really Means," Oct. 1975

Thomas S. Monson, "How Do We Show Our Love?" Jan. 1998

Lawrence Heywood, "A Real Neighbor," July 1974

Thomas S. Monson, "The Way of the Master," May 1996

Russell M. Nelson, "Love Thy Neighbor," Jan. 1987

NOTES:

charity
↑
brotherly kindness
↑
godliness
↑
patience
↑
temperance
↑
knowledge
↑
virtue
↑
faith
add to your

2 Peter 1:5-7

charity
↑
brotherly kindness
↑
godliness
↑
patience
↑
temperance
↑
knowledge
↑
virtue
↑
faith
add to your

2 Peter 1:5-7

charity
↑
brotherly kindness
↑
godliness
↑
patience
↑
temperance
↑
knowledge
↑
virtue
↑
faith
add to your

2 Peter 1:5-7

LESSON THREE

OUR TESTIMONY OF JESUS CHRIST

Hymns

"I Believe in Christ" — Hymns #134
"I Want to Be a Missionary Now" — Children's Songbook #168
"Search, Ponder, and Pray" — Children's Songbook #109
"Testimony" — Hymns #137
"'Twas Witnessed in the Morning Sky" — Hymns #12

SUMMARY:

The last sentence President George Albert Smith uttered before his death was his testifying witness of the Savior! Jesus Christ was not just a good man, effective teacher, or inspiring leader, but the redeemer of the world. As members of the Church, we believe not only that the Savior lived on this earth and died for our sins but also that He still lives! Our lives should reflect those beliefs. Our actions should testify to all that we know He is coming again soon.

Our understanding of the divine mission of Jesus Christ should compel us to action, to show greater love and kindness, and to share His gospel with others. The gospel isn't good news; it's *great* news! We should live our lives so that there will be absolutely no question that Mormons are Christians. Feasting daily on the scriptures and sincere prayer will fill us with hope, joy, and a powerful testimony. By following Jesus Christ, we can return to live with our eternal Father.

QUOTES:

- "You cannot force spiritual things. A testimony is not thrust upon you; it grows. And a testimony is a testimony, and it should be respected, whether it is small or large. We become taller in our testimony like we grow in physical stature and hardly know it is happening, because it comes by growth" (Boyd K. Packer, "How Does the Spirit Speak to Us?," *New Era,* Feb. 2010, 3).
- "Each of us has the responsibility to know the Lord, love Him, follow Him, serve Him, teach and testify of Him" (Russell M. Nelson, "Jesus the Christ: Our Master and More," *Ensign,* Apr. 2000, 4–17).
- "The soul that comes unto Christ dwells within a personal fortress, a veritable palace of perfect peace" (Jeffrey R. Holland, "Come Unto Me," *Ensign,* Apr. 1998, 16–23).

GOSPEL ART:

Isaiah Writes of Christ's Birth – 113
The Nativity – 201
Jesus Praying in Gethsemane – 227
The Crucifixion – 230
The Empty Tomb – 245
Samuel the Lamanite on the Wall – 314
Jesus Christ Appears to the Nephites – 315
The First Vision – 403
Blessing the Sacrament – 603
Missionaries Teach the Gospel of Jesus Christ – 612

VIDEOS:

- "A Light Unto All: A Christmas Gift," www.youtube.com/watch?v=PxKas2Mcjg4
- "The Mediator," http://lds.org/library/display/0,4945,6635-1-4786-2,00.html
- "How do Mormons view Christ?" http://lds.org/library/display/0,4945,6635-1-4786-6,00.html
- "To This End Was I Born," http://lds.org/media-library/video/new-testament-presentations?lang=eng

OBJECT LESSONS:

- Ask someone to draw a picture of a horse or temple or something complicated. Now give them a pattern to trace to draw the same thing. Jesus is our pattern to show us how to create our lives here on earth so that we can live an eternal life with Father in Heaven.
- Show the class some different kinds of keys: old-fashioned ones, key rings, hotel card keys, and so on. Explain how the keys let you into appealing locations: fancy hotel rooms, luxury vehicles, bank safes, and so on. Some people judge their lives by the keys they possess: An education is the key to a good career. A car is a key to geographical freedom. A good job is the key to power and wealth. A large home represents success and security. There is only one key that opens the most important destination of all: Jesus Christ is the key to eternal life with Father in Heaven.
- Show objects that the class has to relate to Jesus Christ

  —Porch light: serves as a beacon to help us find our way home

  —Campfire: provides warmth and comfort

—Lighthouse: offers light in the darkness and perspective in the storm
—Night-light: banishes darkness and eliminates fear
—Car headlights: let us know where we are heading
—Lights in a movie theater: are guides that can be followed
—Lightbulb: inspires us and brings us new understanding

ENSIGN ARTICLES:

Joseph B. Wirthlin, "Spiritual Bonfires of Testimony," Nov. 2002
Lynn M. Schlick, "I Knew We Needed to Find the Book," Mar. 2002, 68
M. Russell Ballard, "Pure Testimony," Nov. 2004
Donald L Staheli, "Securing Our Testimonies," Nov. 2004
Richard G Scott, "The Power of a Strong Testimony," Nov. 2001
Ezra Taft Benson, "Five Marks of the Divinity of Jesus Christ," Dec. 2001
Ezra Taft Benson, "Jesus Christ: Our Savior and Redeemer," June 1990
Russell M. Nelson, "Jesus the Christ: Our Master and More," Apr. 2000
Orson F. Whitney, "The Divinity of Jesus Christ," Dec. 2003
Neal A. Maxwell, "Put Your Shoulder to the Wheel," May 1998

NOTES:

Each of us has the responsibility to know the Lord, love Him, follow Him, serve Him, teach and testify of Him.
Russell M. Nelson

Each of us has the responsibility to know the Lord, love Him, follow Him, serve Him, teach and testify of Him.
Russell M. Nelson

LESSON FOUR

THE PROPHET JOSEPH SMITH, GOD'S INSTRUMENT IN RESTORING THE TRUTH

Hymns

"An Angel Came to Joseph Smith" — Children's Songbook #86a
"Does the Journey Seem Long?" — Hymns #127
"Joseph Smith's First Prayer" — Hymns #26
"Praise to the Man" — Hymns #27

SUMMARY:

President George Albert Smith boldly defended Joseph Smith, saying, "Many of the benefits and blessings that have come to me have come through that man who gave his life for the gospel of Jesus Christ." Every member of the Church has to decide for herself what she believes about the Prophet Joseph, as it is the pivotal point of our religion. Every member can find that out by doing what he did—going to the Lord in earnest, sincere prayer. By praying about the truthfulness of the Book of Mormon, the fruit of Joseph Smith's ministry, we can know if he truly was a prophet of the Lord sent to restore the fulness of the gospel in these latter days.

Through Joseph Smith, all the keys and ordinances required for our salvation were restored to earth. Through Joseph's experiences and writings, we have a greater understanding of the nature of God and our relationship to Him. The young prophet gave his life for his testimony of the Savior; we should be willing to live our lives, testifying to others about what happened in that sacred grove of trees and in our own hearts.

QUOTES:

- "No testimony is more significant to us in our time than the witness of Joseph Smith. He was the prophet chosen to restore the ancient Church of Christ in this, the last time when the gospel will be on the earth before the return of Jesus Christ. Like all the prophets who opened the work of God in their dispensations, Joseph was given especially clear and powerful prophetic experiences to prepare the world for the Savior's Second Coming" (Robert D. Hales, "Seeking to Know God, Our Heavenly Father, and His Son, Jesus Christ," *Ensign*, Nov. 2009, 30).
- "Like Joseph, we must search the scriptures and pray. For many, this means overcoming feelings of doubt and unworthiness, being humble, and learning to exercise faith" (Robert D. Hales, "Receiving a Testimony of the Restored Gospel of Jesus Christ," *Ensign*, Nov. 2003, 28–29).
- "The more I know of the Prophet Joseph, the more I love him, the more I yearn to follow his example, the more I appreciate what our Father in Heaven and His Son have done in restoring this gospel that is destined to fill the earth in these, the latter days" (Joseph B. Wirthlin, "Growing into the Priesthood," *Ensign*, Nov. 1999, 41).

GOSPEL ART:

The Bible and Book of Mormon: Two Witnesses – 326
The Prophet Joseph Smith – 401
Joseph Smith Seeks Wisdom in the Bible – 402
The First Vision – 403
Joseph Smith Receives the Gold Plates – 406

John the Baptist Conferring the Aaronic Priesthood – 407
Melchizedek Priesthood Restoration – 408
Translating the Book of Mormon – 416
Elijah Restores the Power to Seal Families for Eternity – 417

VIDEOS:

- "Answers to Life's Great Questions," http://mormon.org/videos?gclid=CNjCl9fnsasCFZBb7AodCm04iA
- "A Search for Truth," http://lds.org/library/display/0,4945,6635-1-4786-3,00.html
- "Joseph Smith: Prophet of the Restoration," http://lds.org/library/display/0,4945,6635-1-4786-3,00.html
- "Martrydom of Joseph Smith," http://lds.org/library/display/0,4945,6635-1-4786-3,00.html
- "The Restoration," http://lds.org/media-library/video?lang=eng

OBJECT LESSONS:

- Ask someone to bend an old, thick stick. (They shouldn't be able to do it.) Now ask someone to bend a thin, young stick. The Lord needed someone teachable and flexible to restore His kingdom on earth; the Lord needed the young boy Joseph.
- Tell the class you're going to show pictures of different kinds of cars and that they're supposed to raise their hands when they see a car that represents the kind of person they are (sports car, truck, minivan, race car, luxury sedan, taxi, and so on). Explain that all cars get old and eventually break down. Age, accidents,

and everyday use will wear a car out. Sooner or later, all cars are destined for the junkyard unless someone restores them.

In some ways, our lives are like the cars. Just as all cars break down, all people share a common problem that causes us to wear out and eventually die. Just as a car can't fix its own dent or flat tires, we can't fix the problem of death. The Savior keeps our cars running in good condition. He sends mechanics (prophets) who know how to restore cars (us) to their best state when they get old and rusty too.

- Invite someone to play a hymn or song on the piano, but tape down most of the piano keys. After the death of the early apostles, the authority was lost and the fulness of the gospel was not on earth. Explain that there are many wonderful churches on earth today that have some of the piano keys to enjoy but that the Church of Jesus Christ allows us to enjoy the whole song as it was intended—the fulness of the gospel.

ENSIGN ARTICLES:

Dallin H Oaks, "Joseph, the Man and the Prophet," May 1996
Gordon B. Hinckley, "What Hath God Wrought through His Servant Joseph!," Jan. 1997
Neal A. Maxwell, "The Wondrous Restoration," Apr. 2003
Charles Didier, "The Message of the Restoration," Nov. 2003

NOTES:

The more I know of the Prophet Joseph, the more I love him, the more I yearn to follow his example, the more I appreciate what our Father in Heaven and His Son have done in restoring this gospel that is destined to fill the earth in these, the latter days.

Joseph B. Wirthlin

The more I know of the Prophet Joseph, the more I love him, the more I yearn to follow his example, the more I appreciate what our Father in Heaven and His Son have done in restoring this gospel that is destined to fill the earth in these, the latter days.

Joseph B. Wirthlin

LESSON FIVE

THE HOLY PRIESTHOOD—FOR THE BLESSING OF GOD'S CHILDREN

Hymns

"A Young Man Prepared" — Children's Songbook #166
"God of Power, God of Right" — Hymns #20
"O Thou, Before the World Began" — Hymns #189
"Praise to the Man" — Hymns #27
"The Priesthood Is Restored" — Children's Songbook #89

SUMMARY:

When the Savior established His church during His earthly ministry, He chose humble men to serve as His apostles. When He needed to restore His gospel in latter days, He did it through a humble young boy. The Lord always looks for the humble in spirit to bear His priesthood and to lead His Church.

Good men and women of all religions are blessed, but without correct divine authority, they cannot receive saving ordinances and attain a celestial glory. As women, we can inspire priesthood holders around us to honor their priesthood power and use it to bless others' lives.

The priesthood is the power and authority of God given to righteous men to enable them to act in God's name for the salvation of the human family. Earthly ordinances, such as baptism, confirmation, the administration of the sacrament, and temple marriage, need to be performed by the correct priesthood authority in order to be valid in the eyes of the Lord.

QUOTES:

- "The priesthood of God gives light to his children in this dark and troubled world. Through priesthood power, we can receive the gift of the Holy Ghost to lead us to truth, testimony, and revelation. This gift is available on an equal basis to men, women, and children. Through the blessings of the priesthood, we can be equipped with 'the whole armour of God, that [we] may be able to stand against the wiles of the devil' (see Eph. 6:11–18). This protection is available to every one of us" (Robert D. Hales, "Blessings of the Priesthood," *Ensign*, Nov. 1995, 32).
- "The priesthood is intricately woven into who we are and have ever been. As sons and daughters of God, we each have unique responsibilities and roles, and through the blessings of the priesthood, we are all given equal partnership, gifts, and blessings" (Julie B. Beck, "An Outpouring of Blessings," *Ensign*, May 2006, 11).
- "There is no power on the earth like it. Its authority extends beyond life, through the veil of death, to the eternities ahead. It is everlasting in its consequences" (Gordon B. Hinckley, "The Cornerstones of Our Faith," *Ensign*, Nov. 1984, 52–53).

GOSPEL ART:

Moses Calls Aaron to the Ministry – 108
John the Baptist Baptizing Jesus – 208
Christ Ordaining the Apostles – 211
Jesus Blessing Jairus's Daughter – 215
John the Baptist Conferring the Aaronic Priesthood – 407
Melchizedek Priesthood Restoration – 408

Elijah Restores the Power to Seal Families for Eternity – 417
Blessing the Sacrament –603
Administering to the Sick – 613
Home Teaching – 614

VIDEOS:

- "Elder Perry on Priesthood" (4 parts), http://lds.org/media-library/video/prophets-and-apostles-speak-today?lang=eng&start=13&end=24
- "Restoration of the Priesthood," http://lds.org/media-library/video/our-faith?lang=eng
- "Message from Brother David L. Beck," http://lds.org/media-library/video/strength-of-youth-media?lang=eng&start=13&end=24#2010-12-22-message-from-brother-david-l-beck

OBJECT LESSONS:

- Take a lock and attach a sign to it that says "Eternal Life." Explain that the only way to get "Eternal Life" is if you unlock the lock. Give several keys to a class member and have each sister take one and pass the rest to the person next to her, continuing until the keys are gone. Discuss how the keys of the priesthood are passed from one individual to another worthy individual. Once the keys are passed, ask a person without a key to unlock the lock to gain eternal life. She will not be able to because she doesn't have a key. Then give the lock to the person who has the correct key. Discuss how ordinances need to be performed by the correct authority or else they cannot open the lock of eternal life.

- Ask someone in the class to hold an umbrella and keep someone in the class dry from the pretend rain that is falling. Note that the umbrella only needs to be held by one person, but both people are kept dry from the rain. So it is with the priesthood: while only men can hold the priesthood, it is meant to be used to bless everyone and keep us all protected from the storms of earthly life.

ENSIGN ARTICLES:

Robert D. Hales, "Blessings of the Priesthood," Nov. 1995
Julie Beck, "An Outpouring of Blessings," May 2006
Joy Saunders Lundberg, "The Priesthood: God's Gift of Love," Feb. 1993
Bruce R. McConkie, "The Ten Blessings of the Priesthood," Nov. 1977
Henry B. Eyring, "Faith and the Oath and Covenant of the Priesthood," May 2008
Dallin H. Oaks, "Priesthood Blessings," May 1987
Thomas S. Monson, "The Priesthood—A Sacred Gift," May 2007
Russell M. Nelson, "Honoring the Priesthood," May 1993

NOTES:

THE PRIESTHOOD IS INTRICATELY WOVEN INTO WHO WE ARE AND HAVE EVER BEEN.

As sons and daughters of God, we each have unique responsibilities and roles, and through the blessings of the priesthood, we are all given equal partnership, gifts, and blessings.

— JULIE B. BECK —

THE PRIESTHOOD IS INTRICATELY WOVEN INTO WHO WE ARE AND HAVE EVER BEEN.

As sons and daughters of God, we each have unique responsibilities and roles, and through the blessings of the priesthood, we are all given equal partnership, gifts, and blessings.

— JULIE B. BECK —

THE PRIESTHOOD IS INTRICATELY WOVEN INTO WHO WE ARE AND HAVE EVER BEEN.

As sons and daughters of God, we each have unique responsibilities and roles, and through the blessings of the priesthood, we are all given equal partnership, gifts, and blessings.

— JULIE B. BECK —

LESSON SIX

SUSTAINING THOSE WHOM THE LORD SUSTAINS

Hymns

"Come, Listen to a Prophet's Voice" — Hymns #21
"From Homes of Saints Glad Songs Arise" — Hymns #297
"God Bless Our Prophet Dear" — Hymns #24
"Latter-day Prophets" — Children's Songbook #134
"O Ye Mountains High" — Hymns #34

SUMMARY:

A wise Heavenly Father allows us to learn and grow by helping Him build His kingdom here on earth. He calls leaders to direct the work, and He expects us to support and sustain them. When we raise our hand in church to sustain people in their callings, we are testifying that this is the Lord's church. When we use our hands and get to work to help those we sustain, we witness that we are willing to do our part too.

This church, which bears the sacred name of Jesus Christ, is directed by Him. While the Church's leaders are human and imperfect, they speak for the Lord and represent Him in Church matters.

God communicates to His people through a living prophet, a man called through priesthood authority to represent Him. The prophet is also the President of the Church of Jesus Christ of Latter-day Saints and holds the keys of the kingdom on earth. The prophet receives revelation for the Church and leads the administration of priesthood ordinances. He is also called a seer and revelator. By following the Lord's chosen mouthpiece, we will never be led astray.

QUOTES:

- "We always know who is called to lead or to teach and have the opportunity to sustain or to oppose the action. It did not come as an invention of man but was set out in the revelations: 'It shall not be given to anyone to go forth to preach my gospel, or to build up my church, except he be ordained by someone who has authority, and it is known to the church that he has authority and has been regularly ordained by the heads of the church' (D&C 42:11). In this way, the Church is protected from any imposter who would take over a quorum, ward, stake, or the Church" (Boyd K. Packer, "The Weak and the Simple of the Church," *Ensign*, Nov. 2007, 6).
- "A prophet . . . is the authorized representative of the Lord. While the world may not recognize him, the important requirement is that God speaks through him" (A. Theodore Tuttle, "What is a Living Prophet?," *Ensign*, July 1973, 18–20).
- "Sustaining support of prophets, seers, and revelators is not in the upraised hand alone, but more so in our courage, testimony, and faith to listen to, heed, and follow them" (Dennis B. Neuenschwander, "Living Prophets, Seers, and Revelators," *Ensign*, Nov. 2000, 40–42).

GOSPEL ART:

Moses Calls Aaron to the Ministry – 108
Calling of the Fishermen – 209
Christ Ordaining the Apostles – 211
Christ with Three Nephite Disciples – 324
Latter-day Prophets – 506
The Prophet Joseph Smith – 401

John the Baptist Conferring the Aaronic Priesthood – 407
Elijah Restores the Power to Seal Families for Eternity – 417
Sustaining Our Leaders – 610
The Bishop – 611

VIDEOS:

- "Watchmen on the Tower," http://lds.org/library/display/0,4945,6635-1-4786-3,00.html
- "Testimonies of the Apostles," http://lds.org/media-library/video/prophets-and-apostles-speak-today?lang=eng

OBJECT LESSONS:

- Tell the class that a coin represents ancient and modern prophets. Ask them which side of the coin is more important. Then ask if the two sides of the coin can be separated. Explain that both sides of the coin work together for the same purpose, just as all prophets throughout the ages have had the common goal of bringing their people to Jesus Christ.
- Gift wrap two boxes. Leave one empty and put some treats in the other one. Tell the class that one of the boxes has something special in it, while the other one has nothing. Ask a volunteer to choose a box. Let the volunteer see what's inside the box and ask the class if they want her to decide for them. Of course they'll say yes because she now knows what's in both boxes. We follow the prophet because he has "seen what's in the box" of life! He knows what choices we need to make in order to receive eternal rewards.

- Hold a peanut with the shell in your hand behind your back and tell the class that you're holding something that has never been seen by human eyes before. Of course, they won't believe you. Ask for some volunteers to take a peek and tell the class if what you're saying is true or not. When they testify that you're telling the truth, ask how many believe now that there are witnesses. Some still won't. (They must be nuts.) Talk about how the prophets have "seen" and testify of truth. Some in the world will refuse to believe them. Will you?

ENSIGN ARTICLES:

Marie K. Hafen, "Sustaining—and Being Sustained by—the Priesthood," Mar. 1987

Janette Hales Beckham, "Sustaining the Living Prophets," May 1996

James E. Faust, "Called and Chosen," Nov. 2005

Gordon B. Hinckley, "God Is at the Helm," May 1994

Diane K. Jennings, "Sustaining, Supporting, and Surviving—As the Wife of a Busy Church Worker," Oct. 1980

F. Michael Watson, "His Servants, the Prophets," May 2009

David B. Haight, "A Prophet Chosen of the Lord," May 1986

Jeffrey R. Holland, "My Words . . . Never Cease," May 2008

Jeffrey R. Holland, "Prophets in the Land Again," Nov. 2006

Dieter F. Uchtdorf, "Heeding the Voice of the Prophets," July 2008

Gordon B. Hinckley, "We Thank Thee, O God, For a Prophet," Sept. 1991

NOTES:

Sustaining support of prophets, seers, and revelators is not in the upraised hand alone, but more so in our courage, testimony, and faith to listen to, heed, and follow them.

Dennis B. Neuenschwander

Sustaining support of prophets, seers, and revelators is not in the upraised hand alone, but more so in our courage, testimony, and faith to listen to, heed, and follow them.

Dennis B. Neuenschwander

LESSON SEVEN

THE IMMORTALITY OF THE SOUL

Hymns

"Go Forth with Faith" — Hymns #263
"Lead Me into Life Eternal" — Hymns #45
"Lord, Accept into Thy Kingdom" — Hymns #236
"Press Forward, Saints" — Hymns #81
"We Are Marching On to Glory" — Hymns #225

SUMMARY:

This earth life is a part of eternity! We lived before we arrived here and we have somewhere wonderful to go after this mortal experience. What a comfort it is to know that death is only an end of this part of our immortal journey. Our earth life is to prepare us not to die, but to live with our Heavenly Father for eternity. Knowing that everything we do and learn here in life will enhance our experience after we leave this earth should inspire us to do our best while here.

The plan of happiness has been designed to make us happy! Thanks to the resurrection of Jesus Christ, everyone will have an opportunity to step past death and continue living. After our mortal bodies have been purified, our immortal spirits will be housed in them again to live forever. This mortal life is only a temporary home.

QUOTES:

- "Eternal life is to live with our Father and with our families forevermore. Should not this promise be the greatest incentive to do the best within our reach and give the best of ourselves in pursuit of what has been promised to us?" (Jorge F. Zeballos, "Attempting the Impossible," *Ensign*, Nov. 2009, 33).
- "God has known you individually, brethren, for a long, long time (see D&C 93:23). He has loved you for a long, long time. He not only knows the names of all the stars (see Psalm 147:4; Isaiah 40:26); He knows your names and all your heartaches and your joys! By the way, you have never seen an immortal star; they finally expire. But seated by you tonight are immortal individuals—imperfect but who are, nevertheless, 'trying to be like Jesus'!" (Neal A. Maxwell, "Remember How Merciful the Lord Hath Been," *Ensign*, May 2004, 46).
- "When we understand the plan of salvation, we also understand the purpose and effect of the commandments God has given His children" (Dallin H. Oaks, "The Great Plan of Happiness," *Ensign*, Nov. 1993, 72–75).
- "The plan of salvation . . . comprises all of the laws, ordinances, principles, and doctrines required to complete our mortal journey and progress to a state of exaltation enjoyed by our Father in Heaven" (Duane B. Gerrard, "The Plan of Salvation: A Flight Plan for Life," *Ensign*, Nov. 1997, 77–78).

GOSPEL ART:

The Crucifixion – 230
The Resurrected Jesus Christ – 239
The Empty Tomb – 245
Jesus Christ Appears to the Nephites – 315

The First Vision – 403
John the Baptist Conferring the Aaronic Priesthood – 407
Elijah Restores the Power to Seal Families for Eternity – 417
Nauvoo Illinois Temple – 501
Temple Baptismal Font – 504
Young Couple Going to the Temple – 609

VIDEOS:

- "The Plan of Salvation," http://lds.org/library/display/0,4945,6635-1-4786-3,00.html
- "Preparation for the Afterlife," http://lds.org/media-library/video/our-values?lang=eng
- "What Happens When I Die?," http://lds.org/media-library/video/our-faith?lang=eng
- "Chapter 1: Before the Old Testament," http://lds.org/media-library/video/old-testament-stories?lang=eng
- "Man's Search for Happiness," http://www.youtube.com/watch?v=ojX172jF9-I
- "Film of Man's Search for Happiness," http://www.youtube.com/watch?v=cNm1enzlwvo

OBJECT LESSONS:

- Hang a clothesline across the front of the classroom, placing signs that identify the premortal world, mortality, death, spirit prison, paradise, the final judgment, and the three degrees of glory. Create paper dolls that could be hung along the eternal continuum, explaining different kinds of scenarios for each doll's "life," such as when they lived and died and what kind of life they lived. Have the class decide where to hang the paper dolls.

- Ask the class if they would like to eat a cookie now or have five cookies in half an hour. Explain that heaven is like that. Although the things of this world seem very appealing, our heavenly reward is much better. We need to be patient and wait because there is a delicious banquet in store for us after this earth life! Serve cookies at the end of the class.

ENSIGN ARTICLES:

John M. Madsen, "Eternal Life through Jesus Christ," May 2002
Delbert L. Stapley, "The Path to Eternal Life," Jan. 1974
Russell M. Nelson, "Life After Life," May 1987
M. Russell Ballard, "Answers to Life's Questions," May 1995, 22–24
Richard G. Scott, "The Joy of Living the Great Plan of Happiness," Nov. 1996, 73–75
Duane B. Gerrard, "The Plan of Salvation: A Flight Plan for Life," Nov. 1997, 77–78
Neal A. Maxwell, "The Great Plan of the Eternal God," May 1984, 21–23
Dallin H. Oaks, "The Great Plan of Happiness," Nov. 1993, 72–75

NOTES:

When we understand the plan of salvation, we also understand the purpose and effect of the commandments God has given His children.

— Dallin H. Oaks —

When we understand the plan of salvation, we also understand the purpose and effect of the commandments God has given His children.

— Dallin H. Oaks —

LESSON EIGHT

TEMPLE BLESSINGS FOR OURSELVES AND OUR ANCESTORS

Hymns

"Beautiful Zion, Built Above" — Hymns #44
"Families Can Be Together Forever" — Hymns #300
"God Is in His Holy Temple" — Hymns #132
"Holy Temples on Mount Zion" — Hymns #289
"Turn Your Hearts" — Hymns #291

SUMMARY:

Sacred temples are built as a school for the saints to receive eternal ordinances, make important covenants, and gain vital knowledge that will bind their families together forever and allow them to enter the celestial kingdom. A merciful Father in Heaven allows us to receive those endowments for our kindred dead and make eternal blessings available to our ancestors who were not able to enter the temple for themselves.

Salvation is given to every living man and woman, but exaltation requires that everyone be baptized and receive temple ordinances. For those who have lived on earth without hearing the gospel and receiving the saving ordinances, others can perform their temple work. Our ancestors gave us the gift of life, and by doing their temple work, we can help them gain eternal life.

As we research our family history to identify our ancestors, the Lord will help us. He wants families to be together and has given us the tools we need as well as the sacred houses where we can be sealed. It is one of the most important works we can do here on earth.

QUOTES:

- "There exists a righteous unity between the temple and the home. Understanding the eternal nature of the temple will draw you to your family; understanding the eternal nature of the family will draw you to the temple" (Gary E. Stevenson, "Sacred Homes, Sacred Temples," *Ensign*, May 2009, 102).

- "In the ordinances of the temple, the foundations of the eternal family are sealed in place" (Howard W. Hunter, "A Temple-Motivated People," *Ensign*, Feb. 1995, 2).

- "Genealogies, family stories, historical accounts, and traditions . . . form a bridge between past and future and bind generations together in ways that no other keepsake can" (Dennis B. Neuenschwander, "Bridges and Eternal Keepsakes," *Ensign*, May 1999, 83).

- "[The Lord] has trusted you by letting you hear the gospel in your lifetime, giving you the chance to accept the obligation to offer it to those of your ancestors who did not have your priceless opportunity. . . . He offered them an infinite sacrifice. He will love and appreciate those who paid whatever price they could to allow their ancestors to choose His offer of eternal life" (Henry B. Eyring, "Hearts Bound Together," *Ensign*, May 2005, 79).

GOSPEL ART:

Temple Used Anciently – 118
Boy Jesus in the Temple – 205
Elijah Restores the Power to Seal Families for Eternity – 417
Kirtland Temple – 500

Nauvoo Illinois Temple – 501
Salt Lake Temple – 502
Temple Baptismal Font – 504
Washington DC Temple – 505
Young Couple Going to the Temple – 609
The Bishop – 611

VIDEOS:

- "The Blessings of the Temple," http://lds.org/media-library/video/mormon-messages?lang=eng#2009-02-04-the-message-of-the-restoration
- "Why Mormons Do Family History," http://lds.org/media-library/video/our-values?lang=eng
- "Why Mormons Build Temples," http://lds.org/media-library/video/our-faith?lang=eng&start=13&end=24
- "Eternal Family" (several on this page), http://lds.org/media-library/video/truth-restored?lang=eng&start=25&end=36
- "Faith and Families," http://lds.org/media-library/video/ces-firesides?lang=eng#2005-02-01-faith-and-families

OBJECT LESSONS:

- Show the class several items (or pictures of items): candy, coins, a twenty-dollar bill, a stuffed animal, a diamond ring. Ask the class which item they think a baby would be most interested in (candy and the toy). Ask why the baby wouldn't select the most expensive item. (She doesn't understand the value of it.) Talk about how some people don't understand the value of temples, so they make choices that might prevent them from being worthy to enter the temple.

- Invite your ward Family History Specialist to share some special experiences about binding heaven with earth.

- Get two large envelopes, one with a picture of a temple on the outside. Ask a volunteer to place paper dolls inside the two envelopes, creating families out of the pictures. Lick the envelope that has the picture of a temple on the outside. Talk about life's challenges that can tear us apart and then put the two envelopes upside down, shaking the contents around. The family that has been "sealed together" will stay together, but the pictures of the other family will all fall out of the envelope.

ENSIGN ARTICLES:

Russell M Nelson, "Prepare for Blessings of the Temple," Mar. 2002, 17
Howard W. Hunter, "A Temple-Motivated People," Feb. 1995
Richard G. Scott, "Receive the Temple Blessings," May 1999
Howard W. Hunter, "We Have A Work To Do," Mar. 1995, 64–65
Dennis B. Neuenschwander, "Bridges and Eternal Keepsakes," May 1999, 83–85
Dallin H. Oaks, "Family History: In Wisdom and Order," June 1989, 6–8
Boyd K. Packer, "Your Family History: Getting Started," Aug. 2003, 12–17

NOTES:

In the ordinances of the temple, the foundations of the eternal family are sealed in place.

HOWARD W. HUNTER

In the ordinances of the temple, the foundations of the eternal family are sealed in place.

HOWARD W. HUNTER

LESSON NINE

OPEN YOUR SOUL TO THE LORD IN PRAYER

Hymns

"A Child's Prayer" — Children's Songbook #12
"Bless Our Fast, We Pray" — Hymns #138
"Did You Think to Pray?" — Hymns #140
"Joseph Smith's First Prayer" — Hymns #26
"Sweet Hour of Prayer" — Hymns #142

SUMMARY:

One of the most powerful truths we can know is that the Creator of the universe knows and loves us personally. Prayer enables us to talk to our Father who is in heaven as if He were speaking with us face to face here on earth. How wonderful it is not only that God truly hears our prayers but also that He wants to hear them.

Inspired lives include daily personal prayer, family prayer, and, if we are married, companionship prayer. Those prayers should be filled with gratitude and active listening. We should plead for strength, protection, and direction for our families, neighbors, employers, and country's leaders, as well as for the Lord's servants. Families united in prayer can enjoy heaven on earth.

We are commanded to pray always unto the Father and only Him. We can pray either vocally or silently, confessing our sins, showing gratitude, and requesting specific blessings. God answers our prayers by granting us increased ability or by inspiring others to help us. As we pray, we draw closer to our Heavenly Father until our will is the same as His.

QUOTES:

- "Our Father in Heaven has promised us peace in times of trial and has provided a way for us to come to Him in our need. He has given us the privilege and power of prayer" (Rex D. Pinegar, "Peace through Prayer," *Ensign*, May 1993, 65–68).
- "A return to the old pattern of prayer, family prayer in the homes of the people, is one of the basic medications that would check the dread disease that is eroding the character of our society" (Gordon B. Hinckley, "The Blessings of Family Prayer," *Ensign*, Feb. 1991, 2–5).
- "Men and women of integrity, character, and purpose have ever recognized a power higher than themselves and have sought through prayer to be guided by such power" (Thomas S. Monson, "The Prayer of Faith," *Ensign*, Aug. 1995, 2).
- "I can think of no greater teaching to our children than that of the power of prayer" (L. Tom Perry, "Our Father Which Art in Heaven," *Ensign*, Nov. 1983, 11–13).

GOSPEL ART:

Daniel in the Lions' Den – 117
Jesus Praying in Gethsemane – 227
Enos Praying – 305
The First Vision – 403
Young Boy Praying – 605
Family Prayer – 606

VIDEOS:

- "And My Soul Hungered," http://lds.org/library/display/0,4945,6635-1-4786-2,00.html
- "How God Talks to Us Today," http://lds.org/media-library/video/our-faith?lang=eng
- "The First Step," https://lds.org/youth/video?lang=eng

OBJECT LESSONS:

- Show a letter that is addressed to someone but doesn't have a postage stamp on it and ask the class why the postman won't deliver it. Read Alma 33:11 and ask why the prayer of Zenos was heard. Explain that the postage stamp represents sincerity. Sincerity is the postage that delivers our letter (prayer) to Heavenly Father.
- Show the class a shaker of pepper and explain that the pepper represents temptations. Shake some of the pepper into a dish with water in it. Read D&C 10:5 and ask the class what we should do when we're tempted. Now show the class a bar of soap and explain that it represents prayer. Invite a volunteer to rub her fingers on the bar of soap and then touch the surface of the water in the dish. (The pepper will move to the sides of the dish.) Brigham Young once said, "Prayer keeps a man from sin, and sin keeps a man from prayer."
- Invite the class to share their experiences of trying to find a moment in their hectic lives for personal prayer. Before the discussion, ask a volunteer in private to keep raising her hand while you ignore her. You could even acknowledge her but tell her you need to say a few more things before she can talk. Finally, when you call on her, have her tell the class of your plan and explain that sometimes our prayers are like that; we do all of the talking and don't let the Lord participate in the discussion!

- As you walk into the room, talk loudly on your mobile phone as if you are talking to a friend. Talk about your plans for the day, the things you need to do, and then ask for advice as though you are talking to a good friend. Ask the class to compare your conversation to prayer. Remind them that talking on a cell phone is different from prayer in the following ways:
  - God is never out of range
  - We never "lose the signal"
  - The battery never runs dead
  - We never run out of minutes
  - We don't have to remember God's number . . . just talk!

ENSIGN ARTICLES:

Dan B. Skoubye, "Enriching Our Prayers," Aug. 2002, 53
Spencer W. Kimball, "Pray Always," Oct. 1981
Richard G. Scott, "Learning To Recognize Answers to Prayer," Nov. 1989
David A. Bednar, "Pray Always," Nov. 2008
Dallin H. Oaks, "The Language of Prayer," May 1993
Russell M. Nelson, "Lessons from the Lord's Prayers," May 2009
James E. Faust, "The Lifeline of Prayer," May 2002
N. Eldon Tanner, "Importance and Efficacy of Prayer," Aug. 1971
Spencer W. Kimball, "Pray Always," Oct. 1981

NOTES:

Pray always, that you may come off conqueror; yea, that you may conquer Satan, and that you may escape the hands of the servants of Satan that do uphold his work.

D&C 10:5

Pray always, that you may come off conqueror; yea, that you may conquer Satan, and that you may escape the hands of the servants of Satan that do uphold his work.

D&C 10:5

LESSON TEN

THE SCRIPTURES, THE MOST VALUABLE LIBRARY IN THE WORLD

Hymns

"As I Search the Holy Scriptures" — Hymns #277
"Book of Mormon Stories" — Children's Songbook #118
"The Books in the Book of Mormon" — Children's Songbook #119
"Search, Ponder, and Pray" — Children's Songbook #109
"Seek the Lord Early" — Children's Songbook #108

SUMMARY:

An earnest desire for truth can create a powerful experience when seeking within the sacred pages of scripture. The Lord has preserved in holy writ the information He knows will help us in mortality and lead us to Him. We can find more comfort and wisdom in the scriptures than in all other books ever written.

As members of the Church, we are so blessed to have additional clarifying scriptures in the Book of Mormon, Doctrine and Covenants, and Pearl of Great Price. The words in the scriptures come from a loving Heavenly Father who wants us to know what is required to enter again into His presence. As parents, it is vital to our children's salvation that we not only introduce them to the scriptures but also show them how to search the scriptures, understand them, ascertain their truthfulness, and apply the teachings to their lives. All scriptures testify of Jesus Christ and are designed to bring us closer to Him. The words from living prophets are also considered scripture.

QUOTES:

- "Through reading the scriptures, we can gain the assurance of the Spirit that that which we read has come of God for the enlightenment, blessing, and joy of His children" (Gordon B. Hinckley, "Feasting Upon the Scriptures," *Ensign*, Dec. 1985, 42–45).
- "Each of us, at some time in our lives, must discover the scriptures for ourselves—and not just discover them once, but rediscover them again and again" (Spencer W. Kimball, "How Rare a Possession—the Scriptures!," *Ensign*, Sept. 1976, 2–5).
- "If you have not already developed the habit of daily scripture study, start now and keep studying in order to be prepared for your responsibilities in this life and in the eternities" (Julie B. Beck, "My Soul Delighteth in the Scriptures," *Ensign*, May 2004, 107–9).
- "As a person studies the words of the Lord and obeys them, he or she draws closer to the Savior and obtains a greater desire to live a righteous life" (Merrill J. Bateman, "Coming Unto Christ by Searching the Scriptures," *Ensign*, Nov. 1992, 27–28).

GOSPEL ART:

Isaiah Writes of Christ's Birth – 113
Mormon Abridging the Plates – 306
Moroni Hides the Plates in the Hill Cumorah – 320
Christ Asks for the Records – 323
The Gold Plates – 325
The Bible and Book of Mormon: Two Witnesses – 326

Joseph Smith Seeks Wisdom in the Bible – 402
Saving the Book of Commandments – 409
Translating the Book of Mormon – 416
Search the Scriptures – 617

VIDEOS:

- "A Book with a Promise," http://mormon.org/videos?gclid=CNjCl9fnsasCFZBb7AodCm04iA
- "King James Bible Anniversary," http://lds.org/media-library/video/prophets-and-apostles-speak-today?lang=eng&start=25&end=36
- "The Scriptures and the Restoration," http://lds.org/media-library/video/ces-firesides?lang=eng#2003-11-05-the-scriptures-and-the-restoration

OBJECT LESSONS:

- Hold up a lollipop or some other piece of candy that has a wrapper. Ask for a volunteer who likes candy. Invite the volunteer to put the candy in her mouth. When she starts to take off the wrapper, say, "I didn't say you could take the wrapper off. I just said you could put it in your mouth." Have her put the candy in her mouth with the wrapper on and ask her how it tastes. Ask her how long she thinks it will take for her saliva to dissolve the wrapper before she can taste the candy. Point out that her saliva has the ability to dissolve the hard candy, but not the wrapper. Talk about how the scriptures are very much like the candy. Because the scriptures were written by the power of the Holy Ghost, they can't be understood unless a person has the help of the Holy Ghost. The mind of man alone does not have the ability to "take off the wrapper." Elder Howard W. Hunter said, "There is nothing more helpful than prayer to open our understanding of the scriptures." Finally, invite the volunteer and the whole class to enjoy some candy (without the wrappers on) during the rest of the lesson.

- Bring a plate of cookies and ask for volunteers to demonstrate different styles of eating: abstain, sample, taste, snack, gorge, nibble, eat, and feast. Now compare those styles to how we study the scriptures, reminding the class that we should "feast upon the words of Christ."
- Show the class two pictures that seem very much alike but have a few differences. Have the class point out the differences. In order to align our life with the Lord's will, we need to follow His example found in the scriptures and change our life to match His model for us.

ENSIGN ARTICLES:

Dallin H. Oaks, "Scripture Reading and Revelation," Jan. 1995
Henry B. Eyring, "A Discussion on Scripture Study," July 2005
Dallin H. Oaks, "Scripture Reading and Revelation," Jan. 1995
Julie B. Beck, "My Soul Delighteth in the Scriptures," May 2004
M. Russell Ballard, "The Miracle of the Holy Bible," May 2007
Ezra Taft Benson, "The Book of Mormon and the Doctrine and Covenants," May 1987

NOTES:

Feast upon
the words
of Christ

Feast upon
the words
of Christ

Feast upon
the words
of Christ

Feast upon
the words
of Christ

Feast upon
the words
of Christ

Feast upon
the words
of Christ

LESSON ELEVEN

REVELATION FROM GOD TO HIS CHILDREN

Hymns

"How Wondrous and Great" — Hymns #267
"Oh, Holy Words of Truth and Love" — Hymns #271
"We Listen to a Prophet's Voice" — Hymns #22
"We Will Sing of Zion" — Hymns #47
"Welcome, Welcome, Sabbath Morning" — Hymns #280

SUMMARY:

A kind and loving Father in Heaven blesses us with revelation through the Holy Ghost to direct us on the right path during life. Revelation to the Church comes through the Lord's appointed prophet. Personal revelation flows to us through inspired prayer, feelings, and thoughts, and is predicated upon our worthiness.

We gain our testimonies and daily instruction from God through revelation. One of our greatest challenges in life is to learn how to recognize the promptings of the Holy Ghost. The more you pray, study the scriptures, and obey the commandments, the more familiar you will become with how the Lord speaks to you.

QUOTES:

- "The spirit of revelation is real—and can and does function in our individual lives and in the Church" (David A. Bednar, "The Spirit of Revelation," *Ensign*, May 2011).
- "Personal revelation is the way we know for ourselves the most important truths of our existence" (Robert D. Hales, "Personal Revelation: The Teachings and Examples of the Prophets," *Ensign*, Nov. 2007).
- "Receiving personal revelation is not a passive process. As we seek such revelations, we must prepare for these sacred experiences. President Spencer W. Kimball told us that 'God reveals himself to people who are prepared for such manifestations'" (L. Lionel Kendrick, "Personal Revelation," *Ensign*, Sept. 1999).

GOSPEL ART:

Moses and the Burning Bush – 107
Jesus at the Door – 237
The Liahona – 302
Joseph Smith Seeks Wisdom in the Bible – 402
The First Vision – 403
John the Baptist Conferring the Aaronic Priesthood – 407
Salt Lake Temple – 502
Latter-day Prophets – 506
The Gift of the Holy Ghost – 602
Family Prayer – 606
Young couple Going to the Temple – 609
Sustaining Our Leaders – 610
Search the Scriptures – 617

VIDEOS:

- "Are the Heavens Sealed?," http://lds.org/library/display/0,4945,6635-1-4786-6,00.html
- "The Spirit of Revelation," http://lds.org/pages/the-spirit-of-revelation-2011-04?lang=eng&query=revelation

OBJECT LESSONS:

- You need two pieces of paper, about 6x4 inches each. At the beginning of the class, explain that you need to cut a hole in a piece of paper big enough to put your head through. Take the first piece of paper and cut a large hole in it, saying "Here is the best I could do. I have cut a hole in this paper, but I am not able to put my head through it." Take the second piece of paper and cut it according to the diagram below, which allows you to fit it over your head. Tell the class that the first piece of paper represents us when we are faced with a problem or a task. We have very limited ability to get things accomplished. The second piece of paper represents the times we get inspiration from God and trust in Him to help us.

1. Fold. 2. Cut along gray lines.
3. Trim fold along gray line.

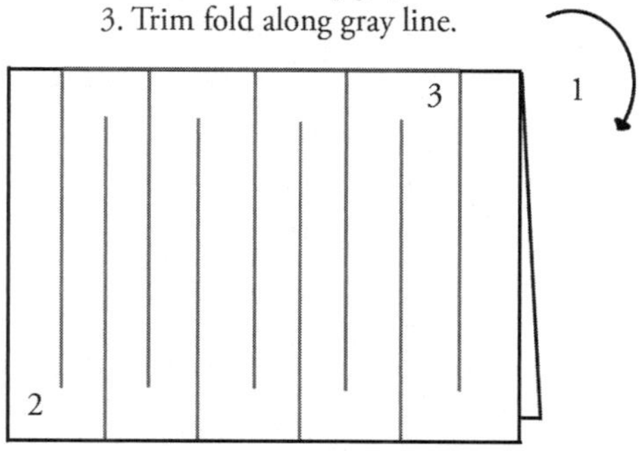

ENSIGN ARTICLES:

Spencer W. Kimball, "Revelation: The Word of the Lord to His Prophets," May 1977.

Bruce R. McConkie, "The Lord's People Receive Revelation," June 1971.

Boyd K. Packer, "Personal Revelation: The Gift, the Test, and the Promise," Nov. 1994

NOTES:

PERSONAL REVELATION is the way we know for ourselves the most important truths of our existence.

ROBERT D. HALES

PERSONAL REVELATION is the way we know for ourselves the most important truths of our existence.

ROBERT D. HALES

LESSON TWELVE

AN ENTHUSIASTIC DESIRE TO SHARE THE GOSPEL

Hymns

"Called to Serve" — Hymns #249
"How Will They Know?" — Children's Songbook #182
"I Hope They Call Me on a Mission" — Children's Songbook #169
"I Want to Be a Missionary Now" — Children's Songbook #168
"What Was Witnessed in the Heavens?" — Hymns #11

SUMMARY:

The most meaningful gift we can give to friends or strangers is the gospel of Jesus Christ. The majority of people on earth do not have an understanding of the Savior and His precious atonement. We have been given the knowledge of saving ordinances, as well as the divinely commissioned authority to provide them to the nations of the earth.

There are many people in the world who are pure in heart and would embrace the fulness of the gospel if they were given the opportunity. As members of the Church, it is our privilege and duty to share the knowledge of life and salvation that we have been blessed with. We are commanded to keep the commandments and then teach them to others. When we truly feel the Savior's love, we have the natural desire to extend it to those around us. When we do, our joy will be felt for eternity. The Lord entrusts us with this important work, and it is our privilege to be a part of it.

QUOTES:

- "For the Savior's mandate to share the gospel to become part of who we are, we need to make member missionary work a way of life" (Quentin L. Cook, "Be a Missionary All Your Life," *Ensign*, Sept. 2008).
- "It is impractical for us to expect that [full-time] missionaries alone can warn the millions in the world. Members must be finders. . . . If we are in tune, the Spirit of the Lord will speak to us and guide us to those with whom we should share the gospel. The Lord will help us if we will but listen" (Spencer W. Kimball, "President Kimball's Vision of Missionary Work," *Ensign*, July 1985).
- "We have long realized that the most potent missionary tool is a good member of the Church" (Gordon B. Hinckley, "A Visit with Elder Gordon B. Hinckley about Missionary Work," *New Era*, June 1973).
- (See more quotes about missionary work in lessons 13, 14, 15.)

GOSPEL ART:

Boy Jesus in the Temple – 205
John Preaching in the Wilderness – 207
Calling of the Fishermen – 209
Go Ye Therefore – 235
Abinadi before King Noah – 308
Alma Baptizes in the Waters of Mormon – 309
Ammon Defends the Flocks of King Lamoni – 310

Four Missionaries to the Lamanites – 418
Missionaries Teach the Gospel of Jesus Christ – 612
Serving One Another – 615

VIDEOS:

- "The Heart and a Willing Mind," http://lds.org/library/display/0,4945,6635-1-4786-3,00.html
- "Church Growth by Stake," http://lds.org/library/display/0,4945,6635-1-4786-7,00.html
- "Why Mormons Send Missionaries Around the World," http://lds.org/media-library/video/our-faith?lang=eng&start=13&end=24
- "Inviting All to Come to Christ," https://lds.org/youth/video?lang=eng
- (See more video suggestions about missionary work in lessons 13, 14, 15.)

OBJECT LESSONS:

- Invite the sisters to be creative in pairs and take turns doing "door approaches" by knocking on the door to your classroom and presenting a gospel message. You'll be amazed at how innovative they'll be!
- Set up a row of dominoes on the front table and then watch the chain reaction as you knock the first one down. Compare that to all of the lives that are touched for good by just one member of the Church being a good missionary.

- Invite the sisters to share their conversion stories.
- (See more object lessons about missionary work in lessons 13, 14, 15.)

ENSIGN ARTICLES:

Earl C. Tingey, "Missionary Service," May 1998, 39–41
Thomas S. Monson, "That All May Hear," May 1995
M. Russell Ballard, "Creating a Gospel-Sharing Home," May 2006
Dallin H. Oaks, "Sharing the Gospel," Nov. 2001

NOTES:

We have long realized that the most potent missionary tool is a good member of the Church.

GORDON B. HINCKLEY

We have long realized that the most potent missionary tool is a good member of the Church.

GORDON B. HINCKLEY

We have long realized that the most potent missionary tool is a good member of the Church.

GORDON B. HINCKLEY

We have long realized that the most potent missionary tool is a good member of the Church.

GORDON B. HINCKLEY

LESSON THIRTEEN

DOING OUR PART TO SHARE THE GOSPEL

Hymns

"Called to Serve" — Hymns #249
"How Will They Know?" — Children's Songbook #182
"I Hope They Call Me on a Mission" — Children's Songbook #169
"I Want to Be a Missionary Now" — Children's Songbook #168
"What Was Witnessed in the Heavens?" — Hymns #11

SUMMARY:

Sharing the gospel with others does not require a formal call or a black name tag. It is our privilege to bring light to a dark world. Our righteous examples can illuminate our neighborhoods and draw the pure in heart to Christ.

When we help prepare young men and women to serve full-time missions and support them with prayers, food, finances, and referrals while they are laboring in the field, the Lord is pleased with our missionary efforts and we will have an even greater desire to open our mouths and share what we know with a world that is seeking truth and direction.

The last command the Savior gave before He ascended up into the heavens was for us to preach the gospel. We become Christlike when we do His work. It is an honor to search for the Lord's lost lambs and to feed His sheep, and we know the Shepherd will return! When we truly feel the Savior's love, it is a natural extension for us to reach out to others and want them to know Him too.

QUOTES:

- "When we received the special blessing of knowledge of the gospel of Jesus Christ and took upon ourselves the name of Christ by entering the waters of baptism, we also accepted the obligation to share the gospel with others" (L. Tom Perry, "The Past Way of Facing the Future," *Ensign*, Nov. 2009, 75).
- "The Standard of Truth has been erected; no unhallowed hand can stop the work from progressing; persecution may rage, mobs may combine, armies may assemble, calumny may defame, but the truth of God will go forth boldly, nobly, and independent till it has penetrated every continent, visited every clime, swept every country, and sounded in every ear, till the purposes of God shall be accomplished and the Great Jehovah shall say the work is done" (Joseph Smith, *Times & Seasons*, 1 Mar. 1842, 709).
- "As Latter-day Saints everywhere, with personal testimonies of these great events, we accept humbly, gratefully, this major responsibility placed upon the Church. . . . Wherever faithful Latter-day Saints are to be found, this spirit of unselfish sacrifice for the greatest cause in all the earth exists. In a statement published to the world during the last world war, the First Presidency of the Church declared: 'No act of ours or of the Church must ever interfere with this God-given mandate'" (Ezra Taft Benson, *Conference Report*, Apr. 1942, 91).
- (See more missionary quotes in lessons 12, 14, 15.)

GOSPEL ART:

John Preaching in the Wilderness – 207
Calling of the Fishermen – 209

The Good Samaritan – 218
Go Ye Therefore – 235
Alma Baptizes in the Waters of Mormon – 309
Ammon Defends the Flocks of King Lamoni – 310
Four Missionaries to the Lamanites – 418
Missionaries Teach the Gospel of Jesus Christ – 612
Serving One Another – 615

VIDEOS:

- "Loving and Serving Others," http://lds.org/service/missionary-service/videos?lang=eng
- "Opportunities for Young Adults," http://lds.org/service/missionary-service/videos?lang=eng
- "Church Growth by Stake," www.lds.org/library/display/0,4945,6635-1-4786-7,00.html
- "The Heart and a Willing Mind," www.lds.org/library/display/0,4945,6635-1-4786-3,00.html
- (See more video suggestions about missionary work in lessons 12, 14, 15.)

OBJECT LESSONS:

- Display a large basket of goodies on the table at the front of the class and begin to eat from it, expressing great delight. Ask the class to share why they love the gospel so much. Continue snacking and then explain that when we enjoy the blessings of the gospel without sharing it with others, it's like you're having a basket of goodies that you love and not sharing it with the class! Pass the basket around and invite everyone to join you in eating yummy treats. At the end of the lesson, ask the sisters how many of them didn't take a treat, ate it right away, or planned on saving it for later. Explain that doing missionary work is similar—even when we share the sweet gospel with others, some people will accept and embrace it, others won't at all, and others might after many years.

- Invite the full-time missionaries to share some conversion stories and experiences with your class.
- (See more object lessons about missionary work in lessons 12, 14, 15.)

ENSIGN ARTICLES:

Dallin H Oaks, "The Role of Members in Conversion," Mar. 2003, 52
Ezra Taft Benson, "President Kimball's Vision of Missionary Work," July 1985
M. Russell Ballard, "Sharing the Gospel Using the Internet," July 2008
Earl C. Tingey, "Missionary Service," May 1998, 39–41
Ronald A. Rasband, "The Divine Call of a Missionary," May 2010
M. Russell Ballard, "Now Is the Time," Nov. 2000
Spencer W. Kimball, "When The World Will Be Converted," Oct. 1984

NOTES:

People I can share the gospel with this week

People I can share the gospel with this week

People I can share the gospel with this week

LESSON FOURTEEN

HOW TO SHARE THE GOSPEL EFFECTIVELY

Hymns

"Called to Serve" — Hymns #249
"Choose the Right" — Hymns #239
"I Hope They Call Me on a Mission" — Children's Songbook #169
"We'll Bring the World His Truth" — Children's Songbook #172
"Ye Simple Souls Who Stray" — Hymns #118

SUMMARY:

As members of the Church who have been blessed with the fulness of the gospel, it is our privilege to help the good people of the world to have an increased understanding of the Savior. In the spirit of love and kindness, our missionary work is about inviting people, not convincing them, to learn more. Rather than debate doctrine with nonbelievers, we gently love them and show them the Savior's love.

The most important part of effective missionary work is not our carefully chosen words, but the Spirit with which we teach. Our desire is to bring greater happiness to others. This is the Lord's work and one of the most important things we can do here on earth.

QUOTES:

- "After all that has been said, the greatest and most important duty is to preach the Gospel" (Joseph Smith, *History of the Church*, 2:478).
- "Great is our work, tremendous is our responsibility in helping to find those to teach. The Lord has laid upon us a mandate to teach the gospel to every creature" (Gordon B. Hinckley, "Find the Lambs, Feed the Sheep," *Ensign*, May 1999, 107).
- "Missionary work is not just one of the 88 keys on a piano that is occasionally played; it is a major chord in a compelling melody that needs to be played continuously throughout our lives if we are to remain in harmony with our commitment to the gospel of Jesus Christ" (Quentin L. Cook, "Be a Missionary All Your Life," *Ensign*, Sept. 2008).
- (See more missionary work quotes in lessons 12, 13, 15.)

GOSPEL ART:

John Preaching in the Wilderness – 207
The Good Samaritan – 218
The Prodigal Son – 220
Go Ye Therefore – 235
Abinadi before King Noah – 308
Alma Baptizes in the Waters of Mormon – 309
Ammon Defends the Flocks of King Lamoni – 310
Four Missionaries to the Lamanites – 418
Missionaries Teach the Gospel of Jesus Christ – 612
Serving One Another – 615

VIDEOS:

- "CongregationalService,"http://lds.org/media-library/video/other-videos?lang=eng
- "Serving From Home," http://lds.org/service/missionary-service/videos?lang=eng
- "Serve When, How and Where You Can," http://lds.org/service/missionary-service/videos?lang=eng
- "A Mighty Change: Conversion," http://lds.org/media-library/video/strength-of-youth-media?lang=eng&start=13&end=24#2010-12-14-a-mighty-change-conversion
- "Sharing the Light of Christ," https://lds.org/youth/video?lang=eng
- (See more video suggestions about missionary work in lessons 12, 13, 15)

OBJECT LESSONS:

- Show the class an old, rotten banana and ask for a volunteer to eat it. (No one will want to.) Ask the class why they don't think it will taste very good. Now hold up a good banana and ask why anyone would choose to eat this one. Explain that our lives are like fruit; people can tell what kind of people we are by the fruit we produce. Matthew 7:20 says, 'Wherefore by their fruits ye shall know them." Ask, "What kind of fruit do you want to produce? You may be the only Book of Mormon people will ever 'read.' Live your lives so that others can tell you're a disciple of Christ and want to know more."
- To illustrate how people follow your actions more than your words, tell the class, "I want you to follow what I say here. Hold your hands up in front of you. Now when I say, 'Go,' clap them together. Let's

start. One . . . two . . . three." (You clap your hands together.) The class will most likely clap their hands together when you do, not when you say "Go." Point out to them that they followed what you did, not what you said. Invite them to live the gospel and not just talk about it.

- Place a hard rock in a bowl of water and explain that it represents the heart of some people. Use a squirt gun to spray some water on the rock to illustrate that when we try to explain the gospel to hard-hearted people, it just rolls off. Show a sponge in the shape of a heart. Use the squirt gun to spray some water on it and point out that the sponge quickly absorbs the water. Some people will soak up the gospel like sponges! Jesus Christ is the Living Water. Not everyone will be ready to accept the gospel, but we still have to offer them the opportunity.
- (See more object lessons about missionary work in lessons 12, 13, 15.)

ENSIGN ARTICLES:

Breanna Olaveson, "Role of Members Important in Sharing the Gospel Online," Sept. 2010

Dallin H. Oaks, "The Role of Members in Conversion," Mar. 2003

NOTES:

After all that has been said, the greatest and most important duty is to preach the Gospel.

Joseph Smith

After all that has been said, the greatest and most important duty is to preach the Gospel.

Joseph Smith

LESSON FIFTEEN

ADVANCING THE WORD OF THE LORD

Hymns

"Called to Serve" — Hymns #249
"Choose the Right" — Hymns #239
"I Hope They Call Me on a Mission" — Children's Songbook #169
"I Want to Be a Missionary Now" — Children's Songbook #168
"We'll Bring the World His Truth" — Children's Songbook #172

SUMMARY:

As we lead others to Christ, we are fulfilling the prophecy that the Church will "[fill] the whole earth" (Daniel 2:35). The careful use of technology enlarges our ability to share the gospel with more people and bless mankind. The Lord opens doors for us as we faithfully strive to spread the Savior's gospel across the globe. Whether we choose to serve a full-time mission or simply blog about our lives in the restored Church, we can bring light into a dark world.

A gracious Father in Heaven invites us to take part in His great work of building His kingdom here on earth by extending callings to us to serve in His church. Whether we serve in the nursery or on the Relief Society General Board, we are valued and invited to partake of His marvelous work and wonder.

QUOTES:

- "When you declare the truth, it will bring an echo, a memory, even if it is an unconscious memory to the investigator, that they have heard this truth before—and of course, they have. A missionary's testimony invokes a great legacy of testimony dating back to the councils in heaven before this world was" (Jeffrey R. Holland, "Missionary Work and the Atonement," *Ensign*, Mar. 2001).
- "When the Spirit is present, people are not offended when you share your feelings about the gospel" (M. Russell Ballard, "We Proclaim the Gospel," *Ensign*, Nov. 1986).

GOSPEL ART:

Daniel Refusing the King's Meat and Wine – 114
John Preaching in the Wilderness – 207
Calling of the Fishermen – 209
The Good Samaritan – 218
Go Ye Therefore – 235
Alma Baptizes in the Waters of Mormon – 309
Four Missionaries to the Lamanites – 418
Missionaries Teach the Gospel of Jesus Christ – 612
Serving One Another – 615

VIDEOS:

- "Inviting All to Come Unto Christ: Sharing the Gospel," http://lds.org/media-library/video/strength-of-youth-media?lang=eng#2010-12-09-inviting-all-to-come-unto-christ-sharing-the-gospel

- "Service Blesses Those Who Serve," http://lds.org/service/missionary-service/videos?lang=eng
- "The Spirit of Compassion," http://lds.org/service/missionary-service/videos?lang=eng

OBJECT LESSONS:

- Place a candy bar on each side of the room. Invite two sisters to come up and link arms, back to back. Tell them they have ten seconds to get their respective candy bar. When you say "Go!" they will each begin pulling the other one in the opposite direction. Either only one will get her candy bar or neither will. Our goal is to return to our heavenly home intact, and it will take all of us working together to accomplish. Once we have the gospel (the candy) we can help others get it too!
- Have the sisters turn on flashlights one at a time. As we bring truth and light to a dark world, it becomes brighter. It all starts with one person; one person can make a difference!
- Put a real flower and an artificial flower in a vase together. Ask the class if they can tell the difference between the two and how they know. Talk about how there are both "real" and "fake" Christians. A fake Christian is one who professes to believe in Christ but doesn't live the gospel. As members of the Church of Jesus Christ, we need to live the gospel so that others will see our religion is "real" and want to know more. Our acts preach stronger sermons than our words.

ENSIGN ARTICLES:

Charles Didier, "Choosing Right When the World Is Wrong," Feb. 2010

Neil L. Andersen, "Whom the Lord Calls, the Lord Qualifies," May 1993

Mark E. Petersen, "Believers and Doers," Nov. 1982

Gordon B. Hinckley, "This Work is Concerned with People," May 1995

Lisa C. Olsen, "New Calling, New Growth," June 1998

NOTES:

When the Spirit is present, people are not offended when you share your feelings about the gospel.

M. Russell Ballard

When the Spirit is present, people are not offended when you share your feelings about the gospel.

M. Russell Ballard

When the Spirit is present, people are not offended when you share your feelings about the gospel.

M. Russell Ballard

When the Spirit is present, people are not offended when you share your feelings about the gospel.

M. Russell Ballard

LESSON SIXTEEN

"OFFER UP THY SACRAMENTS UPON MY HOLY DAY"

Hymns

"As Now We Take the Sacrament" — Hymns #169
"Father in Heaven, We Do Believe" — Hymns #180
"Gently Raise the Sacred Strain" — Hymns #146
"In Memory of the Crucified" — Hymns #190
"The Sacrament" — Children's Songbook #72

SUMMARY:

God ordained the Sabbath to be kept holy and declared it to be a day of rest from our labors. The Sabbath occurs every seven days and is designed to direct our thoughts away from the world and to focus on the Lord instead. In the beginning, God consecrated the seventh day to represent God's day of rest after He created the world. After Christ's resurrection, the first day of the week was honored as the Sabbath to commemorate His resurrection and symbolize that it is the Savior who truly gives us rest.

A helpful guideline in determining whether an activity is appropriate for the Sabbath is to ask the following questions: Will it draw me closer to God? Does it show respect and love for the Savior? Will it inspire me and direct my thoughts to the Lord? The Sabbath day is an opportunity to show the Lord that we put Him first in our lives. The fourth commandment helps us remember our covenants and reevaluate our priorities and weekly activities.

QUOTES:

- "When we partake of the sacrament with a sincere heart, with real intent, forsaking our sins, and renewing our commitment to God, the Lord provides a way whereby sins can be forgiven" (Vaughn J. Featherstone, "Sacrament Meeting and the Sacrament," *Ensign*, Sept. 2001, 23–25).

- "Now is the time to ask ourselves: Is the Sabbath a holy day or a holiday? Shall I worship the Lord or worship pleasures and recreation?" (Charles Didier, "The Sabbath—Holy Day or Holiday?," *Ensign*, Oct. 1994, 26–31).

- "Observance of the Sabbath is not a restriction but a source of strength and protection" (D. Kelly Ogden, "Remember the Sabbath Day," *Ensign*, Apr. 1994, 46–51).

- "Our observance of the Sabbath is an indication of the depth of our conversion and our willingness to keep sacred covenants" (Earl C. Tingey, "The Sabbath Day and Sunday Shopping," *Ensign*, May 1996, 10–12).

- "There is a sure protection for ourselves and our children against the plague of our day. The key to that sure protection surprisingly can be found in Sabbath observance" (James E. Faust, "The Lord's Day," *Ensign*, Nov. 1991, 33–35).

GOSPEL ART:

Jesus Praying in Gethsemane – 227
Salt Lake Tabernacle – 503
Blessing the Sacrament – 603
Passing the Sacrament – 604

Family Prayer – 606
Young Girl Speaking at Church – 607
Family Togetherness – 616
Search the Scriptures – 617

VIDEOS:

- "Remembering the Sacrament," https://lds.org/youth/video/remembering-the-sacrament?lang=eng
- "The Mormon Tabernacle Choir sings 'Sabbath Day,'" http://lds.org/media-library/video/general-conference-april-2011?lang=eng&query=sabbath+day+(collection%3a"media")#2011-04-4002-sabbath-day
- "The Sabbath and the Sacrament," http://lds.org/media-library/video/general-conference-april-2011?lang=eng&query=sabbath+day+(collection%3a"media")#2011-04-1020-elder-l-tom-perry

OBJECT LESSONS:

- Invite someone in the class to enjoy an ice cream sundae with you. Dish out some ice cream and comment on how excited everyone looks about the yummy treat. Now put on various toppings such as pepperoni, barbecue sauce, chopped onions, and grated cheese. The class will probably express disgust. Ask them why they don't want those toppings. They'll probably say that they like those ingredients, but not on top of a sundae. Explain that some of the same activities we do during the week aren't bad activities, but they simply may not be appropriate for the Sabbath day.

- Ask for a volunteer to put some white sugar into a clear glass, representing the Sabbath day (clean and white). Now ask her to add some hot chocolate mix on top, representing the rest of the week. The class will see a definite line, dividing the two colors. Now ask the student to mix them together. The Lord asks us to set apart the Sabbath day to make it different than the rest of the week. The Lord's day should look and feel different from the rest of our week.
- Display a battery-operated flashlight with a weak battery. Talk about how ineffective it is and explain that when our spiritual batteries are recharged every week on the Sabbath, our eternal vision is brighter.

ENSIGN ARTICLES:

Earl C Tingey, "Keeping the Sabbath Day Holy," Feb. 2000, 49
Ezra Taft Benson, "This Is a Day of Sacrifice," May 1979, 32–34
D. Kelly Ogden, "Remember the Sabbath," Apr. 1994
James E. Faust, "The Lord's Day," Nov. 1991
John H. Groberg, "The Power of Keeping the Sabbath Day Holy," Nov. 1984

NOTES:

THINGS I CAN DO ON THE SABBATH

THINGS I CAN DO ON THE SABBATH

THINGS I CAN DO ON THE SABBATH

LESSON SEVENTEEN

THE STRENGTHENING POWER OF FAITH

Hymns

"Be Still, My Soul" — Hymns #124
"Carry On" — Hymns #255
"Choose the Right Way" — Children's Songbook #160
"Dare to Do Right" — Children's Songbook #158
"Do What Is Right" — Hymns #237

SUMMARY:

The first principle of the gospel isn't faith, but faith in the Lord Jesus Christ. Faith is believing in Him with our spiritual eyes when we haven't seen Him with our physical eyes. It is a principle of action that compels us to pray, be obedient, and trust in His promises. We increase our faith by testing and studying His words. Faith has power to move mountains, perform miracles, and prove us worthy to see God.

QUOTES:

- "Choose faith over doubt, choose faith over fear, choose faith over the unknown and the unseen, and choose faith over pessimism" (Richard C. Edgley, "Faith—the Choice Is Yours," *Ensign,* Nov. 2010).

- "We cannot have faith without belief, but we can believe without having faith. Belief is the foundation of faith. Faith is trusting in our Lord and Savior, Jesus Christ" (O. Leslie Stone, "The Constant Exercise of Our Faith," *Ensign*, July 1973).
- "Only faith in the Lord Jesus Christ and His Atonement can bring us peace, hope, and understanding" (Robert D. Hales, "Finding Faith in the Lord Jesus Christ," *Ensign*, Nov. 2004, 70–73).
- "We promote the process of strengthening our faith when we do what is right—increased faith always follows" (L. Whitney Clayton, "Help Thou Mine Unbelief," *Ensign*, Nov. 2001, 28–29).
- "Faith in Jesus Christ takes us beyond mere acceptance of the Savior's identity and existence. It includes having complete confidence in His infinite and eternal redemptive power" (James O. Mason, "Faith in Jesus Christ," *Ensign*, Apr. 2001, 22–27).

GOSPEL ART:

An Angel Saves Abraham – 104
Christ Healing a Blind Man – 213
Jesus Blessing Jairus's Daughter – 215
Jesus at the Door – 237
Christ Walking on the Water – 243
The Liahona – 302
Abinadi before King Noah – 308
Two Thousand Young Warriors – 313
The Brother of Jared Sees the Finger of the Lord – 318
The First Vision – 403

VIDEOS:

- "Finding Faith in Christ," http://lds.org/media-library/video/feature-films?lang=eng
- "Face the Future with Faith," http://lds.org/pages/face-the-future-with-faith?lang=eng&query=faith+(collection%3a"media")
- "Decision by Faith—Jennifer," http://lds.org/media-library/video/truth-restored?lang=eng&query=faith+(collection%3a"media")#2009-04-042-decision-by-faith-jennifer

OBJECT LESSONS:

- Ask for three volunteers. Have the first person blow up a balloon with a tiny bit of air and then pinch the balloon shut with her fingers to hold the air in for a few minutes. The second volunteer blows up her balloon about half full, and the third volunteer blows up her balloon until completely full. Explain that the balloons represent our spirits and the air going in them represents faith. One by one, have each sister unpinch their balloons, allowing them to fly across the room. The first balloon didn't have much faith and couldn't go very far. The third balloon had a lot of faith/air and could really fly, but without much direction. Talk about how we not only have to be "filled" with the Holy Ghost, but also "guided" by the Lord so we'll go in the right direction.
- Hand each person in class a clear marble and ask them to look through it. The image of whatever they're looking at will be upside down. Share Romans 12:2. In today's world, where society calls good evil and evil good, we can have faith that when Christ comes again, all will be transformed to that which is right. Having faith in Jesus Christ helps us see correctly with our spiritual eyes.

- Show the class a checkerboard with 1 grain of wheat on the first square, 2 on the second, 4 on the third, and 8, 16, 32, 64, 128, and so on. Ask the class, "At this rate of doubling every square, how much grain would you have on the checkerboard by the time you reach the sixty-fourth square?" Let the class guess and then tell them the correct answer is enough grain to cover the entire subcontinent of India fifty feet deep! Each square represents some area of their life where they need to trust God. Talk about how our faith may start out small, but as God uses it, the end result can be miraculous and quite powerful!

ENSIGN ARTICLES:

L. Whitney Clayton, "Help Thou Mine Unbelief," Nov. 2001
James O. Mason, "Faith in Jesus Christ," Apr. 2001
John K. Carmack, "Lord, Increase Our Faith," Mar. 2002
Richard G. Scott, "The Transforming Power of Faith and Character," Nov. 2010
Gordon B. Hinckley, "The Miracle of Faith," May 2001
Gordon B. Hinckley, "Faith: The Essence of True Religion," Oct. 1995
Russell M. Nelson, "Faith in Jesus Christ," Mar. 2008
Kevin W. Pearson, "Faith in the Lord Jesus Christ," May 2009
Gordon B. Hinckley, "The Cornerstones of Our Faith," Nov. 1984
Robert D. Hales, "Finding Faith in the Lord Jesus Christ," Nov. 2004
Quentin L. Cook, "Live By Faith and Not by Fear," Nov. 2007

NOTES:

Choose faith over doubt, choose faith over fear, choose faith over the unknown and the unseen, and choose faith over pessimism.

Richard C. Edgley

Choose faith over doubt, choose faith over fear, choose faith over the unknown and the unseen, and choose faith over pessimism.

Richard C. Edgley

Choose faith over doubt, choose faith over fear, choose faith over the unknown and the unseen, and choose faith over pessimism.

Richard C. Edgley

LESSON EIGHTEEN

STAY ON THE LORD'S SIDE OF THE LINE

Hymns

"Arise, O Glorious Zion" — Hymns #40
"As Zion's Youth in Latter Days" — Hymns #256
"Behold! A Royal Army" — Hymns #251
"Do What Is Right" — Hymns #237
"Rise, Ye Saints, and Temples Enter" — Hymns #287

SUMMARY:

President George Albert Smith said that whenever we are tempted, we can ask ourselves, "Which side of the line am I on: the Lord's side or the Devil's?" We will be safe and happy when we stay within the Lord's boundaries. Commandments have been designed by a loving Father in Heaven who knows how to protect us and help us return to live with Him forever. What might seem to be a harsh law is truly tender advice from a concerned Father.

When we obey the Lord's laws, we have the right to claim the blessings associated with that law. Choosing obedience over temptation allows us to feel the Lord's influence in our lives rather than having to maneuver through mortality without His direction. God has given us free agency to make choices and learn how to control our body and spirit so that we can be better prepared to live with Him for eternity.

QUOTES:

- "The Lord has left no doubt in defining His side and where the Saints should be in their thoughts, words, actions, and practices. We have His counsel in the scriptures and in the words of the prophets" (Joseph B. Wirthlin, "The Lord's Side," *Ensign*, Mar. 1993).
- "In this, the dispensation of the fulness of time, as we prepare for the final satanic battles in anticipation of the return of Christ to the earth, it is very important to know who is on the Lord's side. The Lord needs to know on whom He can rely" (Robert C. Oaks, "Who's on the Lord's Side? Who?," *Ensign*, May 2005).
- "If you will remain on the Lord's side of the line, the adversary cannot come there to tempt you" (Charles W. Dahlquist II, "Who's on the Lord's Side?," *Ensign*, May 2007).

GOSPEL ART:

Joseph Resists Potiphar's Wife – 110
Daniel Refusing the King's Meat and Wine – 114
Enoch and His People Are Taken Up to God – 120
Christ and the Rich Young Ruler – 244
The Anti-Nephi-Lehies Burying Their Swords – 311
Captain Moroni Raises the Title of Liberty – 312
Two Thousand Young Warriors – 313

VIDEOS:

- "Can You Imagine?," http://lds.org/library/display/0,4945,6635-1-4786-2,00.html

- "Jesus Christ is the Perfect Example of Obedience," http://lds.org/study/prophets-speak-today/unto-all-the-world/jesus-christ-is-the-perfect-example-of-obedience?lang=eng&query=obedience+(collection%3a"media")
- "Obedience to the Prophets," http://lds.org/media-library/video/general-conference-october-2010?lang=eng&query=obedience+(collection%3a"media")#2010-10-1040-elder-claudio-r-m-costa

OBJECT LESSONS:

- Ask the class if they've ever tried a recipe in a cookbook before. (Most will have.) Then ask the class if they've ever asked a friend for a recipe after tasting a dish she made? Which recipe did they have more confidence in? Why? (They'll respond that they had more confidence in the outcome of their friend's recipe because they tasted the result.) Pass out cookies from a favorite recipe. Explain that the gospel of Jesus Christ is a wonderful recipe for life. We can know that the outcome of believing and following it will be good because of Jesus Christ. When we have "tasted" God's goodness and love, we can have confidence in His plan.
- Give each person a piece of paper and have them draw a line down the middle of it vertically. Invite the class to write on the left side of the paper the characteristics of the natural man, and write on the right side of the page the qualities of Christ. Ask them to write down personal goals for how they can stay on the Lord's side of the line.
- Shine a spotlight or flashlight on a willing volunteer. Now ask her to move one step away. Point out to the class that she may still have a little bit of light on her but not as much as before. Now ask her to move five steps away and show the class that she no longer has any light on her. The light is Jesus Christ. He is not the one who moves from us. It only takes one step away from the Lord to reduce His light

on us. When we sin without repenting, we are taking more and more steps away from Him. To continue to receive the Lord's illumination in our lives, we can't move. We have to stay close to Him!

- Draw a straight line on the floor with masking tape. Ask a volunteer to hold her arms straight out to the side, with both palms facing up, and to walk the length of the line. She should be easily successful. Now, place some heavy books in her hands and ask her to walk the line again. This time it should be more difficult. Explain that the books represent various sins and that it is impossible for us to walk the narrow path with the burden of sin pressing down on us. Have another volunteer help carry the heavy books as they both walk down the line again. Explain that this helper is the Savior and with His support we can successfully complete the tasks of life and the command to be obedient.

ENSIGN ARTICLES:

George R. Hill III, "The Lord's Side of the Line," Aug. 1989
Charles W. Dahlquist II, "Who's On the Lord's Side?," May 2007
Bruce R McConkie, "Be Valiant in the Fight of Faith," Nov. 1974
Joseph B. Wirthlin, "The Lord's Side," Mar. 1993
Lawrence E. Corbridge, "Valiant in the Testimony of Jesus Christ," Sept. 2011

NOTES:

The gospel of Jesus Christ is a wonderful recipe for life.

We can know that the outcome of believing and following it will be good because of Jesus Christ. When we have **"tasted"** God's goodness and love, we can have confidence in His plan.

The gospel of Jesus Christ is a wonderful recipe for life.

We can know that the outcome of believing and following it will be good because of Jesus Christ. When we have **"tasted"** God's goodness and love, we can have confidence in His plan.

The gospel of Jesus Christ is a wonderful recipe for life.

We can know that the outcome of believing and following it will be good because of Jesus Christ. When we have **"tasted"** God's goodness and love, we can have confidence in His plan.

LESSON NINETEEN

TEMPORAL AND SPIRITUAL BLESSINGS FROM THE WORD OF WISDOM

Hymns

"As I Search the Holy Scriptures" — Hymns #277
"For Health and Strength (Round)" — Children's Songbook #21a
"Healthy, Wealthy, and Wise (Round)" — Children's Songbook #280
"Oh, Holy Words of Truth and Love" — Hymns #271
"The Word of Wisdom" — Children's Songbook #154

SUMMARY:

Heavenly Father created us and knows better than anyone what our bodies and spirits need in order to be happy, healthy, and wise. Adhering to the Lord's health code, known as the Word of Wisdom, will bring us both physical and spiritual blessings. Not only does the Word of Wisdom warn us about the harmful substances we should avoid, but it also shows us how to derive greater strength in both body and mind by partaking of good things.

Our bodies and spirits are deeply connected; what we do to the one greatly affects the other. Because of the Savior's infinite atonement, we are able to conquer both spiritual and physical death. When we obey the Word of Wisdom, we feel greater faith and a desire to obey other commandments. The Word of Wisdom enables us to enjoy health in this life and prepares us to live an exalted life.

We are promised spiritual and temporal blessings when we follow the Lord's Law of Health:

- Strength to run and not be weary (D&C 89:20)
- Wisdom and great treasures of knowledge (D&C 89:19)
- Health in your navel and marrow in your bones (D&C 89:18)
- The destroying angel shall pass by you (D&C 89: 21)
- Receive a fulness of joy when spirit and healthy body are united (D&C 93:33–34)

QUOTES:

- "The Word of Wisdom does not promise you perfect health, but it teaches how to keep the body you were born with in the best condition and your mind alert to delicate spiritual promptings" (Boyd K. Packer, "The Word of Wisdom: The Principle and the Promises," *Ensign,* May 1996).
- "The Word of Wisdom is a law—a principle with promise. If we obey the provisions of the law, we receive the promises" (Ezra Taft Benson, "A Principle with a Promise," *Ensign,* May 1983, 53–55).
- "Each day brings more and more evidence showing how important it is to live the Lord's law of health and how dangerous forbidden substances are to our bodies" (Harold G. Hillam, "'Not for the Body,'" *Ensign,* Oct. 2001, 18).
- "While the Word of Wisdom requires strict obedience, in return it promises health, great treasures of knowledge, and that redemption bought for us by the Lamb of God" (Boyd K. Packer, "The Word of Wisdom: The Principle and the Promises," *Ensign,* May 1996, 17–19).

GOSPEL ART:

Daniel Refusing the King's Meat and Wine – 114
Three Men in the Fiery Furnace – 116
Administering to the Sick – 613

VIDEOS:

- "Word of Wisdom," http://lds.org/media-library/video/our-faith?lang=eng&start=13&end=24
- "Daniel," http://lds.org/media-library/video/old-testament-visual-resources?lang=eng
- "Chapter 31: The Word of Wisdom," http://lds.org/media-library/video/doctrine-and-covenants-stories?lang=eng&query=word+wisdom+(collection%3a"media")#2010-06-32-chapter-31-the-word-of-wisdom-february-1833

OBJECT LESSONS:

- Show the class a clean glass of water. Slowly add dirty rocks to the glass, representing unhealthy habits such as smoking, drinking alcohol, eating bad foods, and so on. The dirt from the rocks floats in the glass and the rocks make the glass heavy. Our spirits become weighed down when our bodies aren't clear and clean.
- Invite a doctor or nurse to explain how they must be ready at any time to help save a life if they are paged. Their skills need to be ready at a moment's notice. Compare that to how a man who holds the

priesthood must also be worthy at all times, should he be called to use his priesthood authority to bless someone who is sick or in need. Now compare that to how we need to keep our bodies clear of harmful substances so that we can think clearly and act responsibly at all times. Doctors receive calls on their cell phones when they're needed. Give each sister a colored dot to put on her cell phone to remind her to always keep her body healthy so she can respond to others' needs and feel the Spirit at any given moment.

- Blow up a balloon and tie the end. The balloon represents the body that houses the spirit. Pop the balloon and explain that if we don't take care of our physical bodies, our spirits suffer. Write quotes on slips of paper and place them inside balloons around the room. Throughout the lesson, invite sisters to pop the balloons and read the quotes inside to the class.

ENSIGN ARTICLES:

Joe J. Christensen, "A Reason to Smile," Feb. 2002, 58
Eduardo Ayala, "The Word of Wisdom," Nov. 1990, 10–12
Boyd K. Packer, "The Word of Wisdom: The Principle and the Promises," May 1996
Ezra Taft Benson, "A Principle with a Promise," May 1983
Harold G. Hillam, "Not For The Body," Oct. 2001, 18–21
Russell M. Nelson, "Addiction or Freedom," Nov. 1988, 6–9

NOTES:

While the Word of Wisdom requires strict obedience, in return it promises health, great treasures of knowledge, and that redemption bought for us by the Lamb of God.

—— Boyd K. Packer ——

While the Word of Wisdom requires strict obedience, in return it promises health, great treasures of knowledge, and that redemption bought for us by the Lamb of God.

—— Boyd K. Packer ——

While the Word of Wisdom requires strict obedience, in return it promises health, great treasures of knowledge, and that redemption bought for us by the Lamb of God.

—— Boyd K. Packer ——

LESSON TWENTY

TEMPORAL SALVATION FOR OURSELVES AND OTHERS

Hymns

"Come, Let Us Anew" — Hymns #217
"Glorious Things Are Sung of Zion" — Hymns #48
"Have I Done Any Good?" — Hymns #223
"How Wondrous and Great" — Hymns #267
"Put Your Shoulder to the Wheel" — Hymns #252

SUMMARY:

A part of this life involves learning how to take care of our bodies and spirits so that we will be better prepared to live an exalted life with our Heavenly Father. A merciful Father in Heaven counsels us through His prophets to be prepared in all things. The leaders of the Church have warned us to work for what we have, store a little extra for our times of need, and share what we have with the less fortunate.

Through tithing and fast offerings, we are able to help sustain the Church and bless the nations of the earth. Everything we have in mortality is a test to see if we are able to be good and faithful stewards of even more in eternity.

Work gives us purpose and helps us provide for our wants and needs. Doing our best in work is a matter of integrity, instilling an attitude of honor in all that we do. As mothers, we need to teach our children to work and not rely on others for everything. In order to learn to accept responsibility, children need to see us work, work beside us, and learn to work alone. Idleness is contrary to the gospel.

QUOTES:

- "Self-reliance implies the individual development of skills and abilities and then their application to provide for one's own needs and wants. It further implies that one will achieve those skills through self-discipline and then, through self-restraint and charity, use those skills to bless himself and others" (Marion G. Romney, "Principles of Temporal Salvation," *Ensign*, Apr. 1981).
- "Inspired prophets have always been given laws for their temporal well-being, as well as knowledge that saves eternally. Likewise, as a prelude to this revelation the Lord placed emphasis on both temporal salvation and spiritual salvation: 'All things unto me are spiritual, and not at any time have I given unto you a law which was temporal . . . for my commandments are spiritual' (D&C 29:34–35)" (Roy W. Doxey, "The Lord's People Blessed by Temporal Law," *Liahona*, Oct. 1983).
- "Let us realize that the privilege to work is a gift, that the power to work is a blessing, that love of work is success" (David O. McKay, *Pathways to Happiness* [1957], 381).

GOSPEL ART:

Building the Ark – 102
Noah and the Ark with Animals – 103
Childhood of Jesus Christ – 206
Christ Healing a Blind Man – 213
The Good Samaritan – 218
Christ and the Rich Young Ruler – 244
Lehi and His People Arrive in the Promised Land – 304
Ammon Defends the Flocks of King Lamoni – 310

Helping the Martin Handcart Company across the Sweetwater River – 415

Serving One Another – 615

VIDEOS:

- "Noble Women, Righteous Lives," http://lds.org/library/display/0,4945,6635-1-4786-7,00.html
- "Brazil Helping Hands Ten Year Anniversary," http://lds.org/library/display/0,4945,6635-1-4786-8,00.html
- "We Believe in Doing Good to All Men," http://lds.org/media-library/video/strength-of-youth-media?lang=eng
- "A Desolate Land Blossoms," http://lds.org/media-library/video/75th-welfare-anniversary?lang=eng

OBJECT LESSONS:

- Hold up the hanger and ask what it is used for (hanging up clothes). Ask if anyone can name any other things a hanger can be used for. They might suggest things like

  a. Opening a locked car door
  b. Roasting marshmallows
  c. Cleaning a clogged drain
  d. Craft projects

  Read D&C 60:2 and D&C 82:18. Ask the group what these scriptures have to do with the hanger. Remind everyone that the Lord expects us to do more than just "hang around." Challenge them to use their talents to bless others and improve upon the talents they already have.

- Set out three boxes on the table in the front of the classroom. Ask for three volunteers to each choose a box, but only if they are willing to accept responsibility for it. In one box is a bottle of glass cleaner, requiring the volunteer to wash the window in the classroom. Another box has a bottle of lemon oil, which the volunteer has to use to dust the table or piano in the room. The third box contains a candy bar, which the volunteer gets to eat and enjoy! Explain that we all have our agency to choose whatever we want, but once we have made a choice, we are committed to it, whether it be fun or not.

- Ask a volunteer to make a cake and choose between a wooden spoon or an electric mixer. When we do tasks on our own, it usually takes longer, but if we use a greater power (Heavenly Father), it's easier! His power source can help us accomplish our tasks. Pass out pieces of cake and enjoy!

ENSIGN ARTICLES:

Gordon B Hinckley, "Life's Obligations," May 1999, 3
Marion G. Romney, "Principles of Temporal Salvation," Oct. 1981
H. David Burton, "The Sanctifying Work of Welfare," May 2011
Spencer W. Kimball, "Welfare Services: The Gospel in Action," Nov. 1977

NOTES:

The Lord expects us
to do more than
just "hang around."
D&C 82:18

The Lord expects us
to do more than
just "hang around."
D&C 82:18

The Lord expects us
to do more than
just "hang around."
D&C 82:18

The Lord expects us
to do more than
just "hang around."
D&C 82:18

The Lord expects us
to do more than
just "hang around."
D&C 82:18

The Lord expects us
to do more than
just "hang around."
D&C 82:18

LESSON TWENTY-ONE

THE POWER OF KINDNESS

Hymns

"A Special Gift Is Kindness" — Children's Songbook #145a
"Come Along, Come Along" — Hymns #244
"I'm Trying to Be like Jesus" — Children's Songbook #78
"Kindness Begins with Me" — Children's Songbook #145b
"We Meet Again as Sisters" — Hymns #311

SUMMARY:

The gospel of Jesus Christ can be summed up in one word: love. The Spirit of the Lord is gentle and kind and influences us to do good and be good. We need to be patient with others as they learn and grow, and not look for their faults, just as we hope they would do for us. When we show kindness inside and outside our home, hearts are softened and peace is given to a troubled world.

Charity is the pure love of Christ and the greatest of all virtues. Charity cannot be developed in the abstract; it requires clinical, hands-on experience. It is a process, not an event. Charity is that great feeling we get when we are serving others and comes from a heart filled with pure love. The more we serve others, the more genuine our love will become for others.

QUOTES:

- "Kindness is the essence of greatness and the fundamental characteristic of the noblest men and women I have known. Kindness is a passport that opens doors and fashions friends. It softens hearts and molds relationships that can last lifetimes" (Joseph B. Wirthlin, "The Virtue of Kindness," *Ensign*, May 2005).
- "Real charity is not something you give away; it is something that you acquire and make a part of yourself" (Marvin J. Ashton, "The Tongue Can Be a Sharp Sword," *Ensign*, May 1992, 18–20).
- "I invite you to not only love each other more but love each other better" (Bonnie D. Parkin, "Choosing Charity: That Good Part," *Ensign*, Nov. 2003, 104).
- "We will attain new levels of spirituality and place our lives in closer harmony with Jesus the Christ based on how fully faith, hope, and charity become integral components of our lives" (Joseph B. Wirthlin, "Cultivating Divine Attributes," *Ensign*, Nov. 1998, 25).
- "We all work at feeling joy and finding peace. One of our greatest tools in the process is charity" (Elaine L. Jack, "Strengthened in Charity," *Ensign*, Nov. 1996, 91–93).

GOSPEL ART:

Ruth Gleaning in the Fields – 124
Sermon on the Mount – 212
Christ Healing a Blind Man – 213
Jesus Blessing Jairus's Daughter – 215
The Good Samaritan – 218
The Prodigal Son – 220
Helping the Martin Handcart Company across the Sweetwater River – 415

VIDEOS:

- "The Good Samaritan," http://lds.org/media-library/video/feature-films?lang=eng#1998-05-01-the-good-samaritan
- Video: "Be Not Troubled," www.lds.org/library/display/0,4945,6635-1-4786-3,00.html
- "Lessons I Learned as a Boy," www.lds.org/ldsorg/v/index.jsp?vgnextoid=bd163ca6e9aa3210VgnVCM1000003a94610aRCRD&locale=0

OBJECT LESSONS:

- Introduce the sisters in your Relief Society to several great websites they can go to with their families to choose service projects in their area that will help them reach out to others in their community:

  www.servenet.org
  www.idealist.org
  www.volunteer.com
  www.volunteermatch.org
  www.serve.gov
  www.nationalservice.gov

- Ask a volunteer to hold an ice cube in her hand for the next five minutes. Explain that the ice cube must be held in the same hand in a clenched fist during the whole time. Continue teaching your lesson. After five minutes, ask the class "How difficult was it to pay attention to the lesson when you knew this sister was struggling with her task?" Sometimes we can tell that others are going through a challenge as evidenced by the melting ice, but sometimes all we see is the clenched fist and we don't really know what's going on.
- Set up a little bowling set using empty soda bottles as the pins and a rubber ball. Draw a picture of a woman on the ball and put family members' photos on the "pins." Have someone in the class

roll the ball toward the pins and see how many pins get knocked down. Ask the class how this activity represents our families. When we show kindness (or the opposite) to one person in the family, others are affected. Mothers are very powerful balls, and can have tremendous influence over the atmosphere in the home. An alternate example is to put sticky tape around the ball so that when it touches the pins it connects them (the family) together (kindness) as opposed to knocking the pins down and separating them with unkindness.

- Invite a volunteer to write the word "WORDS" over and over on the chalkboard without separating the letters. Pretty soon the class will see the following: "WORDSWORDSWORDSWORDS." Point out to the class that words can also be swords! Kindness can be in a simple, loving word and holding our tongues when we would be tempted to say something sharp.

ENSIGN ARTICLES:

Joseph B. Wirthlin, "The Virtue of Kindness," May 2005
Milly Day, "Kindness, Goodwill, Generosity," Jan. 1998
Susan Hainsworth, "If You Would Serve Them, Love Them," Mar. 1986
C. Max Caldwell, "Love of Christ," Nov. 1992, 29–30.
Elaine L. Jack, "Strengthened in Charity," Nov. 1996, 91–93
Gene R. Cook, "Charity: Perfect and Everlasting Love," May 2002, 82–83
Bonnie D. Parkin, "Choosing Charity: That Good Part," Nov. 2003, 104–6

NOTES:

I invite you to not only

LOVE EACH OTHER MORE

but

LOVE EACH OTHER BETTER.

Bonnie D. Parkin

I invite you to not only

LOVE EACH OTHER MORE

but

LOVE EACH OTHER BETTER.

Bonnie D. Parkin

I invite you to not only

LOVE EACH OTHER MORE

but

LOVE EACH OTHER BETTER.

Bonnie D. Parkin

I invite you to not only

LOVE EACH OTHER MORE

but

LOVE EACH OTHER BETTER.

Bonnie D. Parkin

LESSON TWENTY-TWO

BRINGING UP CHILDREN IN LIGHT AND TRUTH

Hymns

"Come, Ye Children of the Lord" — Hymns #58
"Dearest Children, God Is Near You" — Hymns #96
"God's Daily Care" — Hymns #306
"I Am a Child of God" — Hymns #301
"Teach Me to Walk in the Light" — Hymns #304

SUMMARY:

While the Church has some excellent gospel instruction provided by seminary, institute, Sunday School, and so on, parents have the ultimate responsibility for raising their children and teaching them truth. Let us not be so caught up in the pursuit of worldly activities that we neglect the spiritual training of our children.

Our faithful examples can help our children see the joy in righteous living so that they desire the same life and blessings. We can bear our testimonies much better with our actions than with our words. We should use not only the designated family home evening time to teach gospel principles but also any time during the day or night when our children's hearts are open. Recent leaders of the Church have warned us that our current home instruction will not be enough to fortify our homes against the adversary in the last days; it is time to clothe them in the armor of God hourly. If we do, our families will be protected and filled with peace, despite the turbulent world that surrounds us.

QUOTES:

- "When our Heavenly Father sends one of his spirit children into a home, it is as if he says to the parents: 'John, Mary, here is my most priceless possession—the soul of a little child. As you can see, he is helpless and completely dependent upon you even for life itself. You are now given the privilege of molding his life as you think best. Please teach him that I am his Father and that Jesus is his Savior and that we want him and you to return and live with us when mortality is over. Remember that I am always available to guide you in rearing this child of ours if you will but seek my help. I hope you will do so often. Your Heavenly Father'" (H. Verlan Andersen, "Bring Up Your Children in Light and Truth," *Ensign*, Nov. 1991).
- "The Lord has given us the charge to 'bring up [our] children in light and truth.' May we respond to this charge with faith and determination to fulfill our duty to the rising generation" (Robert D. Hales, "Our Parental Duty to God and to the Rising Generation," *Ensign*, Aug. 2010).
- "It is not enough simply to provide food and shelter for the physical being. There is an equal responsibility to provide nourishment and direction to the spirit and the mind and the heart. Wrote Paul to Timothy, 'But if any provide not for his own, and specially for those of his own house, he hath denied the faith, and is worse than an infidel' (1 Tim 5:8)" (Gordon B. Hinckley, "Bring Up a Child in the Way He Should Go," *Ensign*, Nov. 1993).

GOSPEL ART:

Adam and Eve Teaching Their Children – 119
Childhood of Jesus Christ – 206

Two Thousand Young Warriors – 313
Joseph Smith Seeks Wisdom in the Bible – 402
Salt Lake Temple – 502
Young Boy Praying – 605
Family Prayer – 606
Young Girl Speaking at Church – 607
Christ and Children from around the World – 608

VIDEOS:

- "Becoming Children of Christ," http://lds.org/library/display/0,4945,6635-1-4786-2,00.html
- "Firm in the Faith of Christ," http://lds.org/library/display/0,4945,6635-1-4786-2,00.html
- "Building Up a Righteous Posterity," http://lds.org/library/display/0,4945,6635-1-4786-9,00.html

OBJECT LESSONS:

- Ask for a volunteer to mold something out of clay. Once she has shown her masterpiece to the class, ask her to mold something out of a flower. Obviously, she won't be able to do that! Tell her to try harder! Explain that we have the power and opportunity to mold our own life but that we can't force our children or spouse to be what they are not. It is fruitless and even damaging to try to mold the flower into something different. Force is not the Lord's plan. Providing the best circumstances for blooming is the Lord's plan.
- Ask for a volunteer to come up to the room to get the absolute best cake in the world. Uncover a plate with a teeny tiny piece on it. Explain that this cake has the finest ingredients in the world.

Ask the class how they feel about quantity versus quality. Are both required in good parenting? How big should our serving of gospel instruction in our homes be for our children?

- Set two buckets on the table in the front of the room, one filled with water and one empty. Ask the class to call out things that make us frustrated or discouraged during a typical day. For each thing they name, take a cup of water out of the full bucket. Explain that we are like that bucket; when things happen during the day that defeat us, a cup of self-esteem and inner peace is taken out. Now, ask the class for suggestions on how we can help a person whose bucket is empty. With each suggestion, pour a cup of water into the empty bucket. Talk about how our homes should be where our buckets are consistently filled each day!

ENSIGN ARTICLES:

H. Verlan Andersen, "Bring Up Your Children in Light and Truth," Nov. 1991

Robert D. Hales, "Our Parental Duty to God and to the Rising Generation," Aug. 2010

Marion G. Romney, "Let Us Set in Order Our Own Houses," Jan. 1985

James E. Faust, "The Greatest Challenge in the World—Good Parenting," Nov. 1990

Gordon B. Hinckley, "Bring Up a Child in the Way He Should Go," Nov. 1993

NOTES:

When our Heavenly Father sends one of his spirit children into a home, it is as if he says to the parents: "John, Mary, here is my most priceless possession—the soul of a little child. As you can see, he is helpless and completely dependent upon you even for life itself. You are now given the privilege of molding his life as you think best. Please teach him that I am his Father and that Jesus is his Savior and that we want him and you to return and live with us when mortality is over. Remember that I am always available to guide you in rearing this child of ours if you will but seek my help. I hope you will do so often. Your Heavenly Father."

H. Verlan Andersen

When our Heavenly Father sends one of his spirit children into a home, it is as if he says to the parents: "John, Mary, here is my most priceless possession—the soul of a little child. As you can see, he is helpless and completely dependent upon you even for life itself. You are now given the privilege of molding his life as you think best. Please teach him that I am his Father and that Jesus is his Savior and that we want him and you to return and live with us when mortality is over. Remember that I am always available to guide you in rearing this child of ours if you will but seek my help. I hope you will do so often. Your Heavenly Father."

H. Verlan Andersen

LESSON TWENTY-THREE

"OF YOU IT IS REQUIRED TO FORGIVE"

Hymns

"Help Me, Dear Father" — Children's Songbook #99
"In Remembrance of Thy Suffering" — Hymns #183
"Lord, We Ask Thee Ere We Part" — Hymns #153
"Reverently and Meekly Now" — Hymns #185
"We Have Partaken of Thy Love" — Hymns #155

SUMMARY:

When we truly understand the gospel of Jesus Christ, we love one another and forgive each other. When we feel anger, bitterness, or hatred toward another person, we will never feel peace, happiness, or the Spirit of the Lord. When we show forgiveness to someone who has wronged us, we are also showing Heavenly Father our gratitude for forgiving us of our transgressions and thanking Him for the atonement, which allows us to repent and be clean once again.

The Church consists of imperfect men and women who are trying to do their best. We may feel especially hurt when someone in the Church has offended us because we expect more from members of the Church, but we need to be careful that both individuals do not lose their testimonies over a negative experience. Letting go of the hurt will allow us to feel the Spirit and fill our hearts with joy, peace, and love.

QUOTES:

- "A spirit of forgiveness and an attitude of love and compassion toward those who may have wronged us is of the very essence of the gospel of Jesus Christ" (Gordon B. Hinckley, "Of You It Is Required to Forgive," *Ensign*, June 1991).
- "A person's ability to forgive is in proportion to the greatness of his soul. Little men cannot forgive" (Richard L. Evans, "The Spoken Word," *New Era*, Mar. 1971).
- "Christ's love was so pure that he gave his life for us: 'Greater love hath no man than this, that a man lay down his life for his friends.' (John 15:13.) But there was another gift he bestowed while he was on the cross, a gift that further measured the magnitude of his great love: he forgave, and asked his Father to forgive, those who persecuted and crucified him" (Marion D. Hanks, "Forgiveness: The Ultimate Form of Love," *Ensign*, Jan. 1974).

GOSPEL ART:

Joseph Is Sold by His Brothers – 109
Sermon on the Mount – 212
The Prodigal Son – 220
The Crucifixion – 230
Nephi Subdues His Rebellious Brothers – 303
The Anti-Nephi-Lehies Burying Their Swords – 311

VIDEOS:

- "My Burden Was Made Light," http://lds.org/family/forgiveness?lang=eng&query=forgiveness+(collection%3a"media")
- "The Third Parable: The Lost Son," http://lds.org/media-library/video/new-testament-stories?lang=eng&query=forgiveness+(collection%3a"media")#2010-11-40-the-third-parable-the-lost-son
- "When Bad Things Happen," http://lds.org/media-library/video/our-faith?lang=eng&query=forgiveness+(collection%3a"media")#2010-05-1170-when-bad-things-happen

OBJECT LESSONS:

- Ask the class who would like the piece of paper in your pocket. No one will be very interested. Now show them a $20 bill and ask the same question. Of course, everyone will be interested now! Ask them why the difference in enthusiasm since the money is just a piece of paper? Tell them you think it must be because it's new. Crumple up the $20 bill and ask who wants it now. Of course, everyone will still want it. Put a pencil mark on it and say to the class, "Now the bill isn't perfect, so I'm sure you won't want it now." Of course, they still will. Tear off a tiny corner and again offer it to the class, saying, "Now it is incomplete and imperfect, so I'm sure you won't want it." Of course, they're still interested. Ask them why they want it. They'll answer that it has a $20 value. Tell them you're going to make it even more valuable by putting it in an envelope. Ask the class how much it's worth now ($20 still). Put it in a fancy box and ask how much the paper is worth now ($20 still). Explain to the class that we're like that $20 bill: We have value no matter if we look perfect, are old and wrinkled, are scarred, or live in a fancy house. God doesn't love us more or less. In our dealings with imperfect people, we need to remember their true value.

- Set out several big blocks or bulky items with signs on them that say "Sin." Ask a volunteer to pick up as many as she can. Once her arms are full, ask her to bend down and pick up a slip of paper on the floor that says "Forgiveness." (It should be difficult for her to do.) Point out to the class that when we are full of sin ourselves, it becomes more difficult to forgive others.

ENSIGN ARTICLES:

Cecil O Samuelson Jr., "Words of Jesus: Forgiveness," Feb. 2003, 48
A. Dean Byrd, "Anticipating the Need to Forgive," Sept. 2011
Gordon B. Hinckley, "Of You It Is Required to Forgive," June 1991
Roderick J. Linton, "The Forgiving Heart," Apr. 1993

NOTES:

A person's ability to forgive is in proportion to the greatness of his soul.
Little men cannot forgive.

Richard L. Evans

A person's ability to forgive is in proportion to the greatness of his soul.
Little men cannot forgive.

Richard L. Evans

A person's ability to forgive is in proportion to the greatness of his soul.
Little men cannot forgive.

Richard L. Evans

LESSON TWENTY-FOUR

RIGHTEOUS LIVING IN PERILOUS TIMES

Hymns

"As Zion's Youth in Latter Days" — Hymns #256
"Choose the Right" — Hymns #239
"Choose the Right Way" — Children's Songbook #160
"Follow the Prophet" — Children's Songbook #110
"How Firm a Foundation" — Hymns #85

SUMMARY:

We have much to do to prepare the world for the Savior's Second Coming. Our homes and values are being assaulted on every side. Still, members of the Church can have a powerful, positive influence if we are not afraid to stand as witnesses of Christ. We can help the pure in heart feel secure as we offer them an anchor against the howling storms.

Relief Society sisters need to be courageous to step into their communities and be an influence for good. The gospel of Jesus Christ is the only thing that will bring peace to the world. We can prevent the adversary from having any power over our homes and hearts by obeying the Lord's commandments, which have been designed to protect us.

QUOTES:

- "Ancient prophets looked with enthusiastic anticipation to our dispensation when the fulness of the gospel would be restored and preached among all nations, and when final preparations would be made for the Second Coming and ultimate reign of the King of Kings, our Savior. Great eternal blessings, keys, and secrets of the gospel, which have been kept 'hid from before the foundation of the world,' were reserved to come forth in this final dispensation to bless our lives. How privileged we are to live in these momentous times!" (J. Lewis Taylor, "I Have a Question," *Ensign*, June 1975).

- "[Satan's] sole purpose is to make you and me as miserable as he is, and the best way for him to accomplish that is to entice us into disobedience. Although there are all kinds of misery in this world, the only kind that is eternal is misery of the soul. And that kind of misery is centered in sin and transgression" (M. Russell Ballard, "When Shall These Things Be?," *Ensign*, Dec. 1996).

- "Paul, in describing our 'perilous times,' did not promise that things would necessarily get easier or necessarily better. He did give counsel to those seeking comfort and assurance in the face of the deteriorating conditions of our day. Just as his prophecies or predictions were clearly accurate, so is his direction to us remarkably relevant as well. Said he, 'Continue . . . in the things which thou hast learned and hast been assured of, knowing of whom thou hast learned them' (2 Tim. 3:14)" (Cecil O. Samuelson Jr., "Perilous Times," *Ensign*, Nov. 2004).

GOSPEL ART:

Three Men in the Fiery Furnace – 116
Daniel in the Lions' Den – 117
Lehi Prophesying to the People of Jerusalem – 300
Captain Moroni Raises the Title of Liberty – 312
Two Thousand Young Warriors – 313
Mormon Bids Farewell to a Once Great Nation – 319
Salt Lake Temple – 502

Young Couple Going to the Temple – 609
The Articles of Faith – 618
My Gospel Standards – 618

VIDEOS:

- "Be Not Troubled," http://lds.org/library/display/0,4945,6635-1-4786-3,00.html
- "Watchmen on the Tower," http://lds.org/library/display/0,4945,6635-1-4786-3,00.html
- "The Whole Armor of God," http://lds.org/library/display/0,4945,6635-1-4786-3,00.html

OBJECT LESSONS:

- Ask the class how many of them like to eat cake. Have them list the ingredients in the cake and ask if they like to eat the raw ingredients separately. Explain that it's a lot like life; separately there are some bitter times; some raw, hurtful times; and some dry, bland times. But there are also good times! God is able to blend them all together to create a life that is meaningful, useful, and tasty! Read Romans 8:28. Explain that the Lord has warned us that perilous times are coming but that they are part of the plan. We need to continue to be righteous and know that He has the best recipe! Pass out pieces of cake to enjoy.
- Read Matthew 5:13. Explain that we are the salt of the earth and that it's pretty easy for us to "lose our flavor" if we don't attend Church, pray, or study the scriptures. Place a salt shaker on the edge of a "Lazy Susan" and spin it slowly at first and then fast

enough that the salt shaker falls off. The perilous days in which we live are represented by the increasing speed of the spinning Lazy Susan. Now, place the salt shaker in the center of the Lazy Susan, and when you spin it, the salt won't fall off. We need to be centered in Christ in order to withstand the difficult times that are ahead.

- Have the class stand up and ask them to jump as high as they can, but with the stipulation that they can't bend their knees. (They won't be able to jump very high.) Then instruct them to jump again, but this time they can bend their knees as low as they want to before launching upwards. Point out to them that the only way to reach and jump high is to bend low first. When we are brought low with trials or difficulties, we must remember that it takes that bending low to propel us higher. If we are brought low with trials, then we can build sufficient faith and trust in God so He can lift us to a higher spiritual place.

ENSIGN ARTICLES:

Richard G. Scott, "The Sustaining Power of Faith in Times of Uncertainty and Testing," May 2003

Cecil O. Samuelson Jr., "Perilous Times," Nov. 2004

Bruce D. Porter, "Defending the Family in a Troubled World," June 2011

L. Tom Perry, "The Tradition of a Balanced, Righteous Life," Aug. 2011

NOTES:

Ancient prophets looked with enthusiastic anticipation to our dispensation when the fulness of the gospel would be restored and preached among all nations, and when final preparations would be made for the Second Coming and ultimate reign of the King of Kings, our Savior. Great eternal blessings, keys, and secrets of the gospel, which have been kept "hid from before the foundation of the world," were reserved to come forth in this final dispensation to bless our lives. How privileged we are to live in these momentous times!

· · · J. LEWIS TAYLOR · · ·

Ancient prophets looked with enthusiastic anticipation to our dispensation when the fulness of the gospel would be restored and preached among all nations, and when final preparations would be made for the Second Coming and ultimate reign of the King of Kings, our Savior. Great eternal blessings, keys, and secrets of the gospel, which have been kept "hid from before the foundation of the world," were reserved to come forth in this final dispensation to bless our lives. How privileged we are to live in these momentous times!

· · · J. LEWIS TAYLOR · · ·

WEBSITE RESOURCES

No need to reinvent the wheel, especially when you're using that wheel to drive on the information superhighway! The Internet is an endless source of ideas, recipes, downloads, crafts, lesson material, music, and instructions for almost anything you'd like to do in your Relief Society Sunday lessons. Just remember, go to the Church's approved material first.

Allow me to give you a serious word of caution about doing online searches. If you enter "Women" into a search engine you will get suggestions for links to all kinds of horrible pornographic web sites. You must type in "LDS Women" or "Relief Society," and even then, look at the description of the site before you click on it! Oh, that the world were as clean and pure as our sweet sisters.

LDS WEBSITE RESOURCES

www.lds.org — The official web site of the Church of Jesus Christ of Latter-day Saints. This should be your first stop on the web.
www.jennysmith.net
www.theideadoor.com/
http://lds.about.com
www.mormons.org
http://of-worth.com
http://www.mormonfind.com
http://www.debanae.net/
www.ldsbrainstorm.com
www.lightplanet.com/mormons
www.mormonmomma.com/gospel/callings
www.ldsworld.com/
www.ldsteach.com
www.lds-living.com
www.JeanniGould.com
www.mormontown.org

www.sugardoodle.net
www.ldsteach.com
www.mormonchic.com
www.ldssplash.com
www.rev-fun.gospel.com
www.thoughts-for-talks.com
www.ldstoday.com
www.shire.net/mormon
www.ldsresources.com
www.zionsearch.com
www.ldslibrary.com
www.ldsmedia.com
www.mormonlinks.com
www.ldsvoices.com
www.ldsprinciples.com

MERCHANDISE

www.lds.org — Official website of the Church of Jesus Christ of Latter-day Saints
www.ldscatalog.com   Order Church materials
www.byubookstore.com
www.ldsweb.org
www.ldsliving.com
www.deseretbook.com
www.seagullbooks.com
www.ctr-ring.com

LDS RELIEF SOCIETY BLOGS

www.hollyscorner.com/blog/lds-resources/relief-society/
www.mormonmomma.com
http://lds.families.com/blog/category/1071
http://segullah.org/daily-special/putting-the-relief-in-relief-society/
http://feastuponthewordblog.org/2009/07/27/coming-up-in-relief-society-and-melchizedek-priesthood-for-2010-and-2011/

http://beliefs.ldsblogs.com/2085/mormon-meetinghouses-relief-society-and-primary-rooms
http://www.ldswomenofgod.com/blog/
http://www.mormonbloggers.com/tag/relief-society

INTERNET GROUPS

I highly recommend that you join a Yahoo Group. It's free to join and you'll meet some of the nicest people around! People share helpful ideas and tips in a real-time setting. You can receive the e-mails individually or as a daily digest. Some groups are more active than others so the quantity of e-mails will vary. No reason to reinvent the wheel when another great Relief Society teacher has already done it out there somewhere!

http://groups.yahoo.com/group/ReliefSociety-L/
http://uk.groups.yahoo.com/group/Relief_SocietyLDS/
http://groups.yahoo.com/group/ldsreliefsocietypresidency/
http://groups.yahoo.com/group/LDSReliefSocietyMeetings/

CLIP ART

I'm thankful for talented artists who share their wonderful creations with me, since I have trouble drawing decent stick people! Here are some of those generous artists:

Most of the web sites mentioned above, plus the following:
www.christysclipart.com
http://www.graphicgarden.com/
www.debanae.net
http://designca.com/lds/
www.coloringbookfun.com
http://www.ldsweb.org/yw_art/yw_clips.html
http://www.davejennings.freeserve.co.uk/clipart/clipart.html
http://primary_art.tripod.com/yw.html
www.jennysmith.net
www.stums.org/closet/html/index.html
http://www.oneil.com.au/lds/pictures.html
http://lds.about.com/library/gallery/clipart/blclipart_gallery_subindex.htm

www.free-clip-art.net
www.ldsfiles.com/clipart
www.coloring.ws/coloring.html
www.apples4theteacher.com

MUSIC

www.lds.org/churchmusic
www.ldsaudio.com
http://defordmusic.com
www.Jennyphillips.com
www.joansowards.com
www.heartrisemusic.com
www.jenmagazine.com/lds-music/lds-music.asp
www.ldsmusicnews.com
http://lds.about.com/library/clipart/blnewera_music_1975.htm
— Great index of all sheet music offered in the *New Era* & *Ensign* magazines from 1975–89.
www.ldsmusicworld.com
www.latterdaysongs.com
www.ldsmusictoday.com
www.musicfreedom.com/ellishadlock
www.markhansenmusic.com
— LDS rock music, downloads, firesides, performances

ABOUT THE AUTHOR

Trina Boice grew up in California and currently lives in Las Vegas. In 2004, she was honored as the California Young Mother of the Year, an award which completely amuses her four sons. She earned two bachelor degrees from BYU, where she competed on the speech and debate team and the ballroom dance team. She was president of the National Honor Society Phi Eta Sigma and served as ASBYU Secretary of Student Community Services.

Trina also studied at the University of Salamanca in Spain and later returned there to serve an LDS mission in Madrid for one and a half years. She has a real estate license, travel agent license, two master degrees, and a black belt in Tae Kwon Do, although she's the first one to admit she'd pass out from fright if she were ever really attacked by a bad guy.

She worked as a legislative assistant for a congressman in Washington, DC, and was given the "Points of Light" Award and Presidential Volunteer Service Award for her domestic and international community service. She wrote a column called "The Boice Box" for a newspaper in Georgia, where she lived for fifteen years. She taught Spanish at a private high school and ran an appraisal business with her husband for twenty years. She currently writes for Homemaking-Cottage.com, 702events .com, LDWMagazine.com, and *Desert Saints Magazine* and is the entertainment news editor at Bella Online. She is the national director of marketing for Multi-Pure Corporation.

Trina was selected by KPBS in San Diego to be a political correspondent during the last presidential election. If she told you what she really did, she'd have to kill you.

A popular and entertaining speaker, Trina is the author of ten books and can't wait to write her next one! You can read more about her books and upcoming events at www.trinaboice.com.

NOTES

0 26575 59308 2